Hold Everything

by

Pam Damour and Betty Mitchell

Who is Pam Damour?

Known as the "Decorating Diva", Pam learned early in life, while spending time on her grandparents' farm, that making something from "scratch" was not only a way of life, but it was the better way of doing things. Holding on to those values, she went from farm to fabric and has had a very successful 30+ year career as an interior designer and sewing professional. Pam offers professional drapery workroom training to the trade and consumers. As a seasoned career speaker, she travels internationally, teaching her specialty techniques that have brought her years of continued business as the "Couture of Home Dec Sewing". She is the author of *Pillow Talk, Cheaper by the Dozen, Got Quilts?, The Tangled Home,* producer of 12 Home Dec DVDs, several patterns, and designer of notions and templates. An interior designer by profession and a quilter by passion, Pam lives on the shore of Lake Champlain in a log home nestled at the foot of the Adirondack Mountains, where she teaches sewing retreats and her Window Treatment Boot Camp. Her down to earth nature, never forgetting her roots, combined with her professionalism, creates a warm and creative experience. To attend one of Pam's events, contact your local sewing store or go to www.pamdamour.com.

From the Author

I still remember the day I met Betty Mitchell. We were at a sewing conference (I know, what a surprise!) in Raleigh, North Carolina. I knew immediately we would become great friends, but I never could have imagined what a great asset she would be to my sewing career. In the thirteen years that we have been friends, she has sewn tirelessly for my last four books, she has pushed my creativity to new limits and has made me a better teacher. Of all my dearest sewing friends, she has inspired me the most. Thank you Betty for your friendship, your advice and your guidance. This book is dedicated to you.

Hugs & Stitches,
Pam

Who is Betty Mitchell?

Betty Mitchell began her love affair with the sewing machine at the age of eight and it has grown ever since. She spent 30 years in Rhode Island, teaching Family and Consumer Sciences and 'retired' to work for sewing machine dealers in southwest Florida for eight years. During that time, she not only sold machines and taught classes, she also spent three years as a store manager for one of the largest dealers in the country. At the same time, she began teaching at national dealer conventions, various sewing and quilting shows, as well as local and regional sewing guilds. Seven years ago, she re-retired to her grandchildren in Kentucky. She still teaches at a couple of local stores and has launched a line of patterns. Originally a garment sewer, she now concentrates more on Home Décor, embroidery, accessories and sergers. Her classes are meant to be informative and relaxing. Betty says, "In the end, it's just a bunch of thread and fiber to have fun with! If there's a sewing tool or fabric that I haven't met, it's not because I haven't tried. I firmly believe that I'll never have enough fabric and I certainly deserve the best tools."

From the Author

Wow! Just wow! Never ever would I have thought I would even consider writing a book let alone already be planning the next one! I have been surprised in so many ways. I found myself 'sewing' in my sleep, 'writing' in my sleep and 'designing' in my sleep and then waking up and having to finish what I had started! Obviously, it's been a 7 month, 24 hour a day adventure! Enjoy what we have created and please use this book to jump start your own creativity!

Thank you, thank you Pam Damour for asking me to co-author this book. It's been an amazing collaboration of creativity and friendship. I am so honored to call you my friend.

Sew in Peace,
Betty

Introduction

PAM DAMOUR THE DECORATING DIVA
495 Point Au Fer Road
Champlain, NY 12919

Photography:
Pam Damour
Betty Mitchell

Cover design, book layout, and index:
Elaine Cloutier

© 2017 Copyright
Pam Damour

All rights reserved including the right o reproduction in whole or in part in any form.

It is illegal and in violation of the copyright laws to share or sell these designs. Respect of the copyright laws protects the designers and thereby assures a steady supply of original designs with high quality digitizing and standards.

Printed in China

This book had been a joy and a curse for me. It's a curse because it's totally out of my comfort zone and has been the most challenging project thus far in my career. It's a joy because I was able to create it with one of my best friends, who challenges and inspires me. In writing this book, Betty and I have tried to provide a variety of bags and projects for everyday use. We have projects from the very easy to the extremely complicated, as indicated by our signature "spools of difficulty". We have used testers to test our projects and critique them, hoping that we have created a book of projects anyone can make. We know we have missed a thing or two and there is sure to be some typos, so please forgive us in advance. One of the things that's new with this book is that we are including several video links to demonstrate what we're trying to show you, and we hope you'll take advantage of these tutorials and find them helpful.

This book has been a labor of love from both me and Betty. Think of it as your launch pad to design and create your own bag patterns. Use the pocket designs, the zipper variations, and the assorted bottoms and corners to create something truly yours. Try some of the new products and notions we have introduced and step outside of your comfort zone!

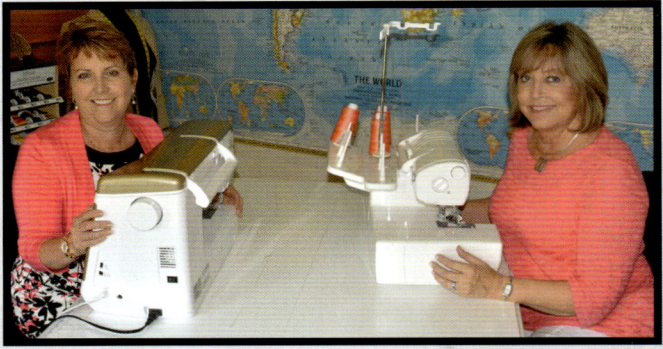

Word of Thanks

There are so many people who helped make this book come together, so I'd like to mention just a few. As always, I want to thank my staff for their never ending support, and my husband Joe who tolerates my crazy work schedule (Only a few more years till retirement honey!) and the revolving door of ladies who come in to help me.

Special thanks to everyone who contributed their ideas, and advice with our projects and this book. They include Diane Murphy, Carolyn Wells, Penny Pombrio, Sue Donahue, Linda Abel, Fran Hershfield, Leigh Lutz, Tammie Gerke, Jaclyn Catrenich, Debbie Burris, Terry Speer, Melody Eichler, Jenny Ashline, Cindy Drolette, Kristin Barkman, Elaine Cloutier and Pinky Dowling.

A special thanks to my models Leah Damour, Lacey Pombrio and Katee Brothers.

Contents

 = Video Tutorials

 = available at pamdamour.com

Whenever you see the camera icon, go to www.pamdamour.com, click on the Video Clips link and you will find the video clips for the techniques in this book.

SAMPLE - DIFFICULTY 2

Each project has spools of difficulty ranging from 1-5.

1 being the easiest, 5 being the most difficult.

Basic Instructions 7	
Embroidery Basics 7	
Continuous Bias 10	
Hardware 12	
Zipper Insertions 16	
Bag Variations 26	
Corners 26	
Pockets 29	
Straps 42	
Great Finishes 47	
Binding 47	
Laminating 52	
Finishing Techniques 54	
Organizers 57	
The Hold Everything Bag 58	
Hold Anything Basket 70	
Macro Wallet 75	
The Cell Phone Wallet 80	
The Mini Wallet 87	
The Pocket Wallet 89	
Quick Clutch Wallet 92	
Evening Clutch 96	
Art Supply Wallet 96	
The Elegant Organizer 97	
The Zipper Pocket Bag 103	
With A Little Help From Our Friends 106	
De-De's Bag 107	
Jaclyn's Bag 112	
Leigh's Yoga Bag 116	

The Melinda Bag 119	
Teacher's Pet 123	
Sew on the Go 130	
Essential Travel & Cosmetic Bags 130	
Travel Roll Up 136	
Grab and Go Make Up Bag 139	
Men's Toiletry Bag 141	
Water Tote 143	
Quick Projects Using Pre-Cuts 147	
Wristlet Key Chain 148	
Zipper Lanyard 149	
Electronics Bag 150	
"Zip It" Eye Glass Case 152	
Strap Wrap 154	
Precut Play 155	
Wine Bag 156	
Bags That Hold More 158	
The New and Improved Expandable Zipper Bag 159	
The Weekender Tote 167	
Wheeled Tote 175	
Acknowledgements 183	
Embroidery 184	
Glossary 185	
Product List 187	
Index 188	

Foreword

Linda Pacini
National Training Manager for
Baby Lock Sewing Machines

I've had the pleasure of working with Pam extensively over the last several years and am always amazed by her wealth of knowledge, boundless energy and how she so freely shares from her years of masterful experience. No stranger to workroom methods, time saving techniques and just an overall better way of doing everything, Pam brings a level of expertise to everything that she does. This book does not disappoint with its many projects and techniques that will make you want to smack your head and say, "Why didn't I think of that!"

If you add only one book this year to your collection with the intention of setting about makings gifts galore, this one is it!

In her role as the National Training Manager for Baby Lock USA, Linda Pacini gets to interact with sewers every day through the video content that she and dozens of other talented sewers provide through Baby Lock's many video channels. Linda is passionate about sewing and recognizes that some of the best advancements in sewing comes from the unique ways that today's sewers approach their projects. Teaching people how to take advantage of time saving techniques and tools and how to grow their sewing skills is her never-ending mission.

Basic Instructions

EMBROIDERY BASICS

Machine Embroidery brings a whole new element to sewing, giving us many opportunities to express ourselves through design and color.

The key to successful embroidery is to use the proper stabilizer for the type of fabric and embroidery designs. Because these designs are not heavily stitched, minimal stabilizing for most of them will work. While there are enough methods of embroidery to write a whole book, these are some of the methods used in this book.

What Type of Stabilizer to Use?

Always check what type of fabric you will be embroidering. The fabric type and density of your design will determine what you should use. I don't claim to be an expert in this field, so I'm going to suggest what works for me.

Fantastic Fusible Fabric Backing

When using silk or fine delicate fabrics, be sure to always prep fabric first with Fantastic Fusible Fabric Backing. This backing will add stability without changing the hand of the fabric. This is a permanent backing. It is also great when embroidering on knits, as it prevents any stretching.

Peel & Stick Stabilizer

There are many fabrics that should not be hooped because of "hoop burn". This is when the hoop might leave a permanent impression on the fabric. For these fabrics, use hooped peel and stick stabilizer.

- After hooping, score paper with a straight pin.

- Pull paper off exposing sticky stabilizer.

- Press fabric into place, smoothing out the entire surface.

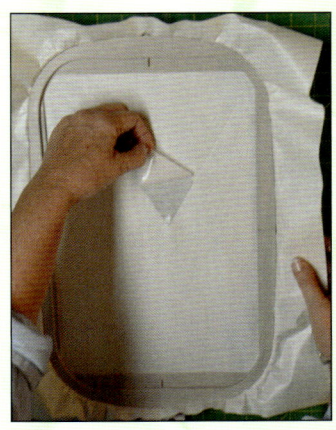

Basic Instructions

EMBROIDERY BASICS (CONTINUED)

Tear Away Stabilizers

Tear away stabilizers can be hooped or used as a floater (an extra layer shoved under the hoop for those dense designs). It tears away clean and adds that extra stability for perfect embroidery. When floating a tear away, basting in the hoop can help hold this stabilizer in place. You may also use a temporary basting spray designed for this purpose.

Wash Away Stabilizers

Wash away stabilizers can be used as a bottom stabilizer or a topper. After embroidering your design, gently tear away any loose stabilizer. Then place your project in lukewarm water and rinse until all the stabilizer is gone. Wash away paper stabilizer can be run through your copier to make paper piecing patterns. The beauty of this is there is no need to tear all the paper away.

Heat Dissolving Stabilizers

Stabilizers that dissolve with heat work great when you can not use water to wash away the stabilizer, but you can use heat. It is the preferred topper for thick pile fabrics. To use, float the stabilizer on the fabric and baste in the hoop before embroidering.

NOTE: Always test your fabric, embroidery thread and stabilizers before proceeding with any embroidery project. When I do my practice stitch-outs, I do them on a large enough piece of fabric to use them in a project if the stitch-out turns out well.

Appliqué Embroidery

When creating an appliqué with your embroidery machine, your first step, once your fabric is hooped and your design is loaded, is to outline stitch your back ground fabric.

- Add appliqué fabric and baste design again.
- Trim away fabric close to the outside of the stitching line.
- Satin stitch design in place once you have trimmed it.

Three Dimensional Embroidery

Supplies

- Wash away stabilizer
- Heat cutting tool
- 40 weight Rayon thread
- Ceramic tile - 8" square or larger
- Embroidery design of your choice

Construction

- Hoop two layers of wash away stabilizer and two layers of nylon organza.
- Place the hoop on the embroidery machine and stitch the embroidery design.

Basic Instructions

EMBROIDERY BASICS (CONTINUED)

Three Dimensional Embroidery (CONTINUED)

Construction (CONTINUED)

- Once the embroidery is complete, remove the hoop from the machine and place the embroidered design on the ceramic tile.

- Place the fine tip on the heat cutting tool and heat for about four minutes.

- With a burn proof surface under your fabric, such as ceramic tile, carefully trace around the outline of the embroidered design to burn away the excess stabilizer with the heat cutting tool. Use a steady movement and do not hesitate. Be careful to keep the tip of the wand next to the outside edge of the design to ensure that you do not burn any area that is not intended to burn away.

- Now you have a perfectly stitched free standing embroidery design ready to be placed on any fabric or surface. Stitch into place either by hand or by machine.

Monogram Embroidery

This book comes with a monogram collection. They are all hand drawn and can be combined and layered. There are two font sizes, 2 $\frac{1}{2}$" and 5". Depending on your machine and its capabilities, you may be able to enlarge and/or reduce them to suit whatever project you're making.

Supplies
- Tear away stabilizer
- Embroidery thread
- Bobbin thread

Construction

- If embroidering something small like a bag pocket, hoop your stabilizer only in the hoop. If your embroidery machine has a "baste in the hoop" feature, use this for pocket placement. If not, use a temporary basting spray like 505 or KK2000 to hold fabric in place.

- After your design is completed, remove any basting stitches and gently remove stabilizer.

Basic Instructions

CONTINUOUS BIAS

Continuous bias is a term that refers to the technique where fabric is sewn into a tube, then cut in a spiral fashion to create bias strips in a very fast and efficient manner. It requires no more fabric than cutting straight grain strips of fabric.

Begin with a square or rectangle of fabric. We're showing a rectangle, as most of the time, your fabric will be rectangular. Remember that a square is just a rectangle with 4 equal sides.

- Trim off a 45° angle of fabric as shown.

- Slide the triangle over to the other side.

- With right sides together, sew the pieces together using a $1/2$" seam allowance.

- Press seam open creating a parallelogram.

- Draw lines on the WRONG side of the fabric, the width of your desired bias strips. Number your strips as shown.

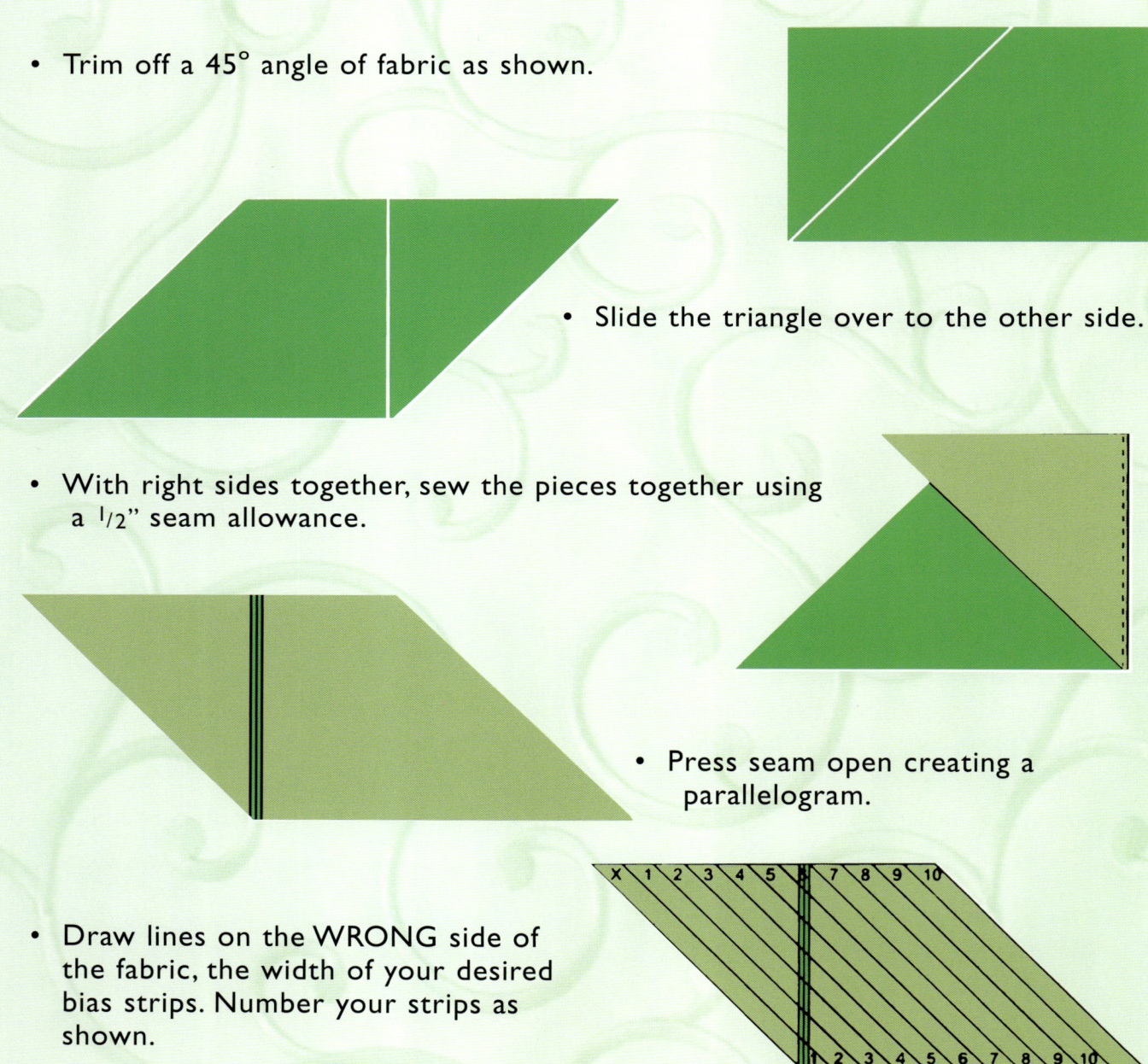

Basic Instructions

CONTINUOUS BIAS (CONTINUED)

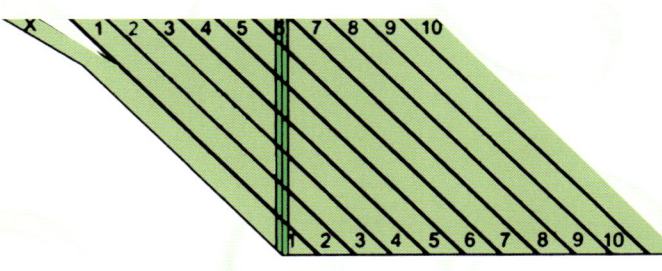

- Cut about 2" on the line between the "X" and #1.

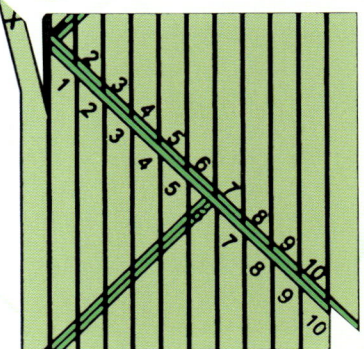

- Line up the numbered strips so the same numbers are together. With right sides together, pin, making sure like numbered strips are aligned and stitch a 1/2" seam. Press all seams open and flat. Cut on the drawn lines to create easy, uniform bias strips.

This bias can be used for single welt cord, double welt cord, ruffles, ruching, shirred welting, bias binding and banding.

MATH FORMULAS FOR CALCULATING CONTINUOUS BIAS

_____ X _____ ÷ _____ = _____ ÷ 36
Length of Bias   Width of Bias   Width of Material   Amount of Inches

= _____
Amount in Yards

OR If you have a piece of fabric and want to know how much bias it will yield:

_____ X _____ ÷ _____ = _____ ÷ 36
Length of Fabric   Width of Fabric   Width of Bias Needed   Total Bias in Inches

= _____
Total Bias in Yards

Basic Instructions / Hardware

CLUTCH & WALLET CLASP FRAMES

Our frames come in different sizes and finishes. At the time this book went to press, we had them in three sizes, in four finishes and some even have an embossed texture. After making these for a few years, I've learned a few tricks to help with their installation.

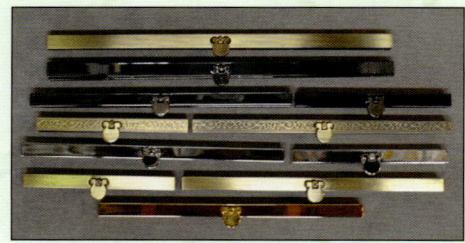

PREP YOUR PROJECT

You will have an easier installation if you prep your project before beginning the installation. If there is excess thickness due to extra layers of fabric or stabilizer, trim away some of the inner layers so that your frame will go on more easily. Serge the top edge, trimming any uneven edges. If you don't have a serger, trim edges evenly and zig-zag.

Supplies

- Hot glue gun with a small tip to get inside the frame (hot and ready to go)
- Iron (hot and ready to go)
- Size 00 Phillips Screwdriver
- Flat Head Screwdriver
- Sharp scissors
- FriXion Pen and/or marking pencils
- Nail polish remover
- Fabric glue
- Wallet Clasp
- Sewing awl or stiletto

BEFORE YOU BEGIN

- Decide which end will have the "female" end of your project and mark where the opening is.

- Cut two snips down about 3/8".

- Peel back outer layers and cut away the inner layers where the clasp opening will go.

- Fold the outer layers inside, covering the raw edges you just cut away.

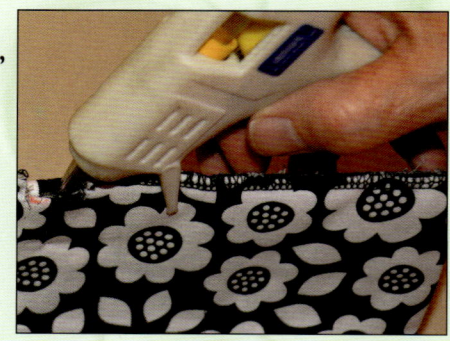

- Add a small amount of hot glue between the two layers to secure.

Basic Instructions / Hardware

CLUTCH & WALLET CLASP FRAMES (CONTINUED)

- With your iron, heat the female end of your frame. This will allow the hot glue to stay soft much longer, giving you the time you need to get your project in place.

- Use your Flat Head Screwdriver to help ease your project into the frame.

- The glue will help keep the fabric in the frame.

- With a size 00 Phillips Head Screwdriver, screw in each of the little screws that came with your frame, until the head of the screw is flush with the metal frame.

- Install the other side of frame by heating frame and adding hot glue.

NOTE: Use the stiletto to make a hole in the fabric. You may want to add a small drop of fabric glue or hot glue in each hole to keep screws secure. Extra screws are available at www.pamdamour.com.

- Remove any hot glue residue on your frame with nail polish remover.

Basic Instructions / Hardware

BAG FEET

Bag feet are used on flat bottom bags to protect the bottom of the bag from getting dirty. They install similar to paper fasteners.

- Fuse the Deco-Magic® to the wrong side of bag bottom, centering, leaving 1/2" seam allowance all the way around.

- If using the Seven Corner Ruler®, mark for the desired corner and trim both bag bottom fabric and Deco-Magic®.

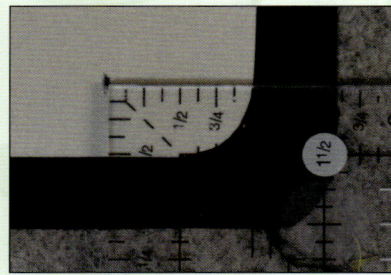

- Measure from each corner of the Deco-Magic®, and mark for your bag feet. Refer to your specific pattern instructions for the positioning of feet. If no measurement is given, put feet 1" from the bag edge.

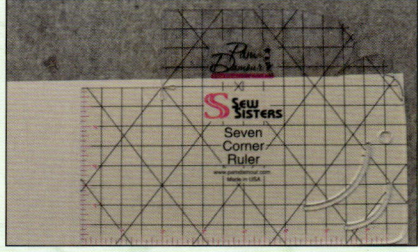

- Use the tip of your seam ripper to cut a 1/4" slot for the prongs of your bag feet.

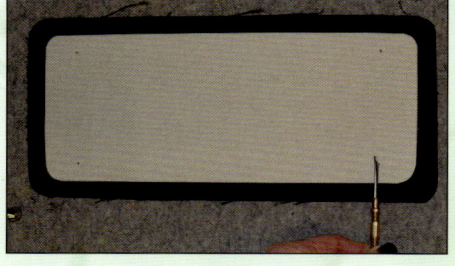

- From the right side, put prongs through slits to the back while going through the back of the plate.

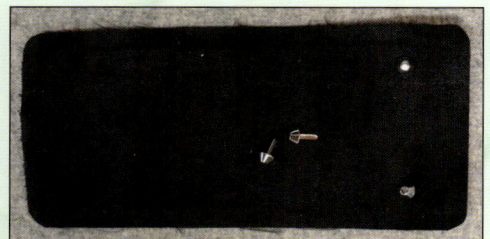

- Open prongs and spread flat to secure.

Basic Instructions / Hardware

KEY FOBS

If you're like me, you don't like constantly digging through your bag to find your keys. Having them in an easy to find spot is a great feature in any bag. You can make a key fob with leftover fabric and a swivel clip, then sew it into the top edge of your bag before finishing it.

Supplies
- Strip of fabric cut 2" x 6" (or zipper tape)
- Swivel clip
- Matching thread

Construction
- Fold your 2" x 6" strip of fabric with raw edges to the center and press.
- Align the two folded edges together and press.
- Top stitch folded edges together.

ZIPPER TAPE KEY FOB

Got some extra zipper tape? Make a key fob!

Supplies
- 6" of zipper tape
- Swivel clip

Construction
- Cut a 6" length of zipper tape and fold in half. Press flat to set the crease in your zipper. Slide zipper through the end of a swivel hook.

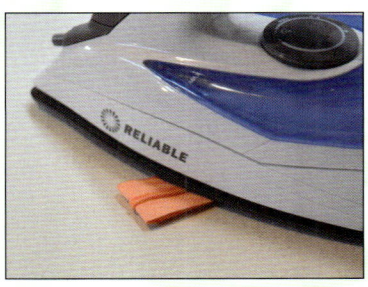

- Sew to the top edge of the bag, along the inside edge.

Basic Instructions / Zippers

DOUBLE ZIPPER CLOSURE

This closure is perfect for that large bag where easy access is a must. Zippers can be used independently, or attached with a zipper tab handle, so one quick pull opens the bag.

Supplies

- Outside fabric, lining fabric and Super Shaping Foam® Single Side Fusible per pattern size requirements
- Two pieces of zipper tape in lengths required by the specific pattern
- 2 zipper slides
- Scraps of coordinating fabric to bind the edges of the closure
- Scraps of lining fabric to create the zipper pull tabs

Construction

All seams are 1/2" unless otherwise noted.

- Stitch a piece of zipper tape to each long side of the center with teeth down. Stitching should be fairly close to the zipper teeth - as close to a 1/2" seam as possible.

- Place the center lining piece on the outside center piece RST and stitch together on top of the stitching that attached the zipper tape.

- Turn right side out and press.

- Topstitch 1/4" from the folded edges next to the zipper teeth.

- You now have an unstitched section of zipper tape on each side of the center strip.

- You also have 2 strips of coordinating fabric and 2 strips of lining fabric that are to be used to finish these edges of the zipper tape. All of these pieces measure 1 1/2" by the length of the center strip.

Basic Instructions / Zippers

DOUBLE ZIPPER CLOSURE (CONTINUED)

Construction

- Place the coordinating fabric strips RST with the zipper tape on the outside of the center strip and stitch a strip to each piece of zipper tape close to the zipper teeth.

- Turn center strip to the back side and place the right sides of the lining fabric strips to the wrong side of the zipper tape. This will sandwich the zipper tape between the two 1 1/2" wide strips on each piece of the zipper tape.

- Stitch the three layers together, stitching on top of the previous stitches.

- Press all strips away from the zipper teeth.

- Topstitch 1/4" from folded edges as you did on the center strip.

- Attach a zipper pull to each piece of the zipper tape.

NOTE: *In order for the zippers to open in the same direction, zipper pulls must each be attached to the same end of the Double Zipper Closure.*

- With the zippers closed and using a 1/4" seam allowance, use French Binding (see page 49) to bind the entire length of the same end of the closure where you attach the zipper pulls. Use a strip of coordinating fabric that is 1 1/4" wide and long enough to cover the closure. The ends of this binding do not need to be finished off as they will be covered when the closure is attached to the bag.

- Pull open the other ends of the zipper tape. You will have three sections - two small side sections and the larger center section.

17

Basic Instructions / Zippers

DOUBLE ZIPPER CLOSURE (CONTINUED)

Construction (CONTINUED)

- Each of these 3 sections needs to be bound. Both ends of the binding on the center strip will need to be turned in to provide a zipper stop and to give a finished look.

- On the smaller side pieces the binding must be finished in the same way at the ends near the zippers and they should be left unfinished at the other side that will attach to the top of the bag.

- Attach Zipper Tabs (see below). Attach a tab on each pull if you wish to be able to open one side at a time or attach one longer tab connecting both pulls to open both sides at the same time.

ZIPPER TABS

Use these instructions to create fabric pulls for your zippers. The same instructions create ties and drawstrings when longer strips of fabric are used.

Supplies

- Fabric strips that are 1" wide. (You will need 10"-12" for a zipper tab.)

Construction

- Pull and press the fabric through a $1/2$" Bias Tape Maker.

- After pressing, fold in half and topstitch into a strip that finishes $1/4$" wide.

NOTE: Straight of grain fabric works just as well as bias fabric when using a Bias Tape Maker.

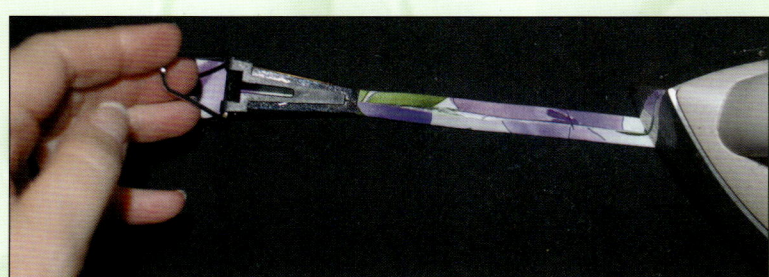

18

Basic Instructions / Zippers

ZIPPERED LINING

Why a zippered lining, you ask? When you make a bag with a separate lining, you have to leave an opening somewhere in the lining to turn the bag right side out. Then you have to hand sew this opening shut. If you put a zipper in the lining, it gives you that opening and you merely close the zipper to close the opening. In addition, it gives you a secret compartment to carry extra cash, hide jewelry or anything you need to keep secure.

Supplies

- Bag lining, cut according to the pattern
- 1 piece of zipper tape cut 1" longer than your desired opening
- 1 zipper slide
- Zipper foot for your sewing machine
- Matching thread

Construction

- Cut your lining out, according to the pattern. If there is a bottom seam, that is usually the best place to put the zipper, but a side seam will work too!

- Separate your zipper and sew one side to each side of your lining, positioning it in your desired location.

- Marry the zipper together, as shown. When you put the slide on, one end will still be open.

- Take the slide all the way off the end, so the entire zipper is closed. Open one end about 3" and reinsert the slide, leaving it in the center, with both ends closed.

Basic Instructions / Zippers

ZIPPERED LINING (CONTINUED)

Construction (CONTINUED)

- Bring the two sides together and complete the seam using a zipper foot and the needle off to the side of the foot.

- Overlap your stitching past the end of the zipper 1/2" on each end.

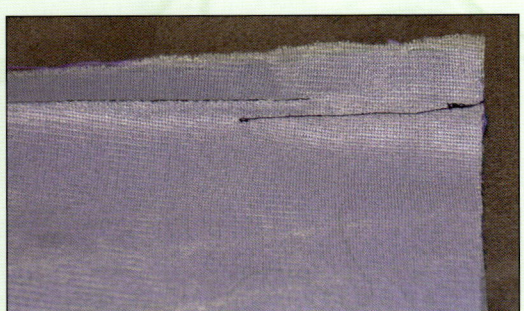

- Press your seam open and flat. Serge or zig-zag edges if bag is to be laundered. Complete the bag lining according to the directions.

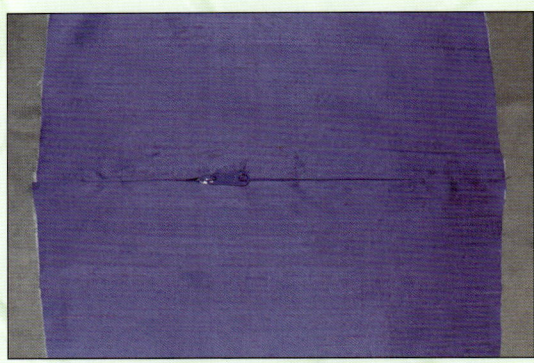

Basic Instructions / Zippers

"BUTTONHOLE" ZIPPER INSERTION

I call this the "Buttonhole" Zipper insertion. Similar to a bound buttonhole, it's the perfect finish for a zipper opening. It can be made just as the opening, or you can make it a pocket too!

Supplies
- Placket fabric
- FriXion Pen
- Zipper tape with 1 slide
- Peel and stick or Décor-Bond® stabilizer

Construction

- With a FriXion Pen, draw your zipper box on the wrong side of your zipper placket. This box should be $1/2$" high by the length of your zipper opening. Cut your zipper tape 1" longer than the box.

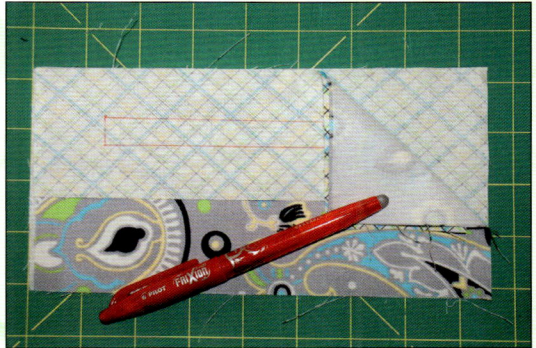

- Make a fabric sandwich with two pieces of pocket fabric, WST. Stabilize the front pocket fabric.

- Place zipper placket on pocket outer fabric, with right sides together.

- Sew along zipper box line, starting and stopping along one of the long sides.

- DO NOT START AND STOP IN A CORNER!

- DO NOT stitch past the box line and then back stitch! If you stitch past, remove the stitches and try it again. This is very important for this opening to be correct.

NOTE: When stitching across the ends of the box, I count my stitches to make sure each end is the same size.

Basic Instructions / Zippers

"BUTTONHOLE" ZIPPER INSERTION (CONTINUED)

- Draw a line down the center and make a "Y" at each end. Cut center line and "Y", cutting all the way to the corner stitch.

- Trim a scant strip of fabric (about the width of 2 threads) on each side of the center cut.

- Pull the placket facing to the back side and pleat as shown.

- The front will look like this.

- Center zipper teeth over opening and stitch in the ditch with a zipper foot. Use basting tape to keep zipper in place.

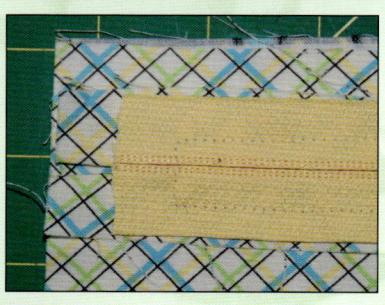

- Trim zipper tape in excess of $1/2$" off the end of the zipper box.

Basic Instructions / Zippers

TWO WAY TOP ZIPPER PLACKET

This technique is a great one to use, especially on larger bags where you want to close the bag but need full access to the inside. Remember, when adding this element to your bag, you have to add extra zipper tape to each end so that the bag opens all the way. The amount that you add depends on the girth of your bag, so measure accordingly. Because of the unique reversible coil of our own Pam Damour brand zippers, two-way zippers are a cinch!

Supplies

- 2 Zipper placket pieces
- Zipper tape
- 2 Zipper slides
- 2- 2" Fabric squares
- Bonash Bonding Powder
- Bonash Pressing Sheet
- Double Piping or Double Welting Foot
- 1/4" Basting tape

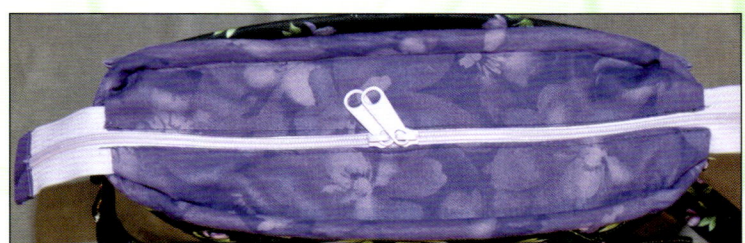

Construction

NOTE: I use Bonash Bonding Powder on my placket to add extra body to soft fabrics, such as quilting cotton. This step is optional.

- Cut two placket pieces to desired size.

- Place fabric on pressing sheet, wrong side up.

- Sprinkle wrong side of fabric with Bonash Bonding Powder and press using folded over pressing sheet. Press for about 10 seconds to melt the powder into the fabric. This will make your fabric fusible.

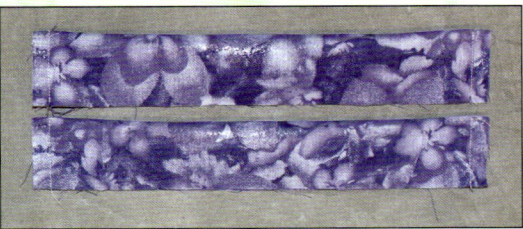

- Fold in half lengthwise, and sew across ends, using a 1/2" seam allowance.

- Turn right sides out and press flat.

Basic Instructions / Zippers

TWO WAY TOP ZIPPER PLACKET (CONTINUED)

Construction (CONTINUED)

- Cut your zipper according to pattern. The zipper will extend past the placket at each end. This excess is necessary for the bag to open completely. If you don't know how long to cut the zipper, allow the same amount of extension for the bottom girth of the bag.

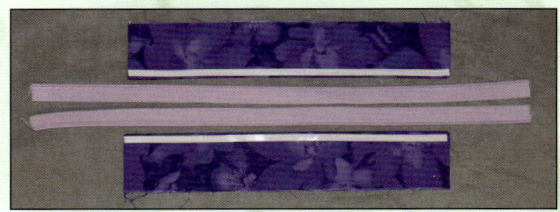

FOR EXAMPLE: *If your bag bottom is 2" wide, add 2" extra to each end of the zipper.*

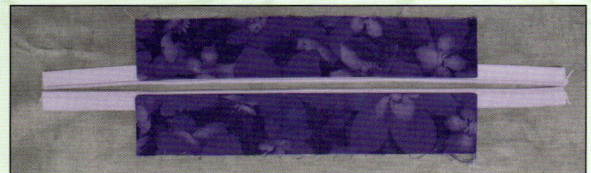

- Add basting tape to folded edge to keep zipper teeth in place. Using the double welting foot, or zipper foot, stitch along the folded edge, back stitching at each end, with the zipper teeth up.

Put zipper slide on each end.

Zipper End Tabs

- Sew 2" tab onto each end of zipper, right side of the fabric to the wrong side of the zipper, press away from the zipper.

- Fold sides in and press.

- Fold end over and press.

- Fold folded edge over and top stitch.

- Pin placket to the top edge of bag and finish according to your specific bag directions.

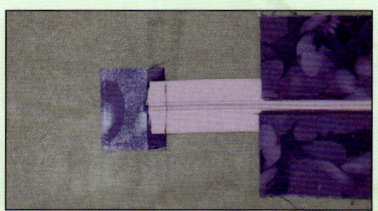
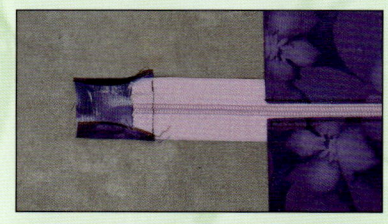
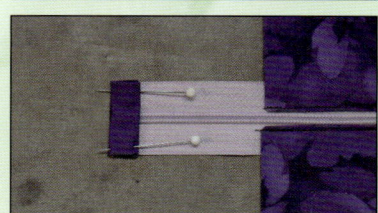

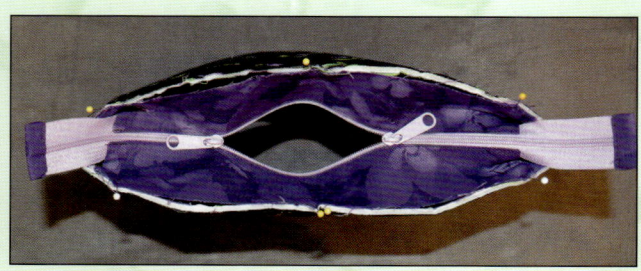

Basic Instructions / Zippers

BASIC ZIPPER INSERTION

Inserting zippers in bags is much like inserting them in pillows or other sewing projects. Using the right zipper design for the project makes the insertion easier.

Supplies

- Zipper foot, piping or double welting foot
- Zipper tape cut to size, including seam allowances.
- One or two zipper slides. Please refer to your pattern for more details.

Construction

- Sew each side of zipper tape onto each side of pocket or zipper opening.

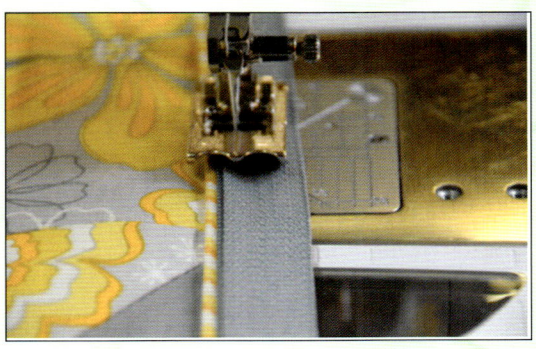

- After sewing each side of the zipper, with RST, it is time to insert the slide.

- You will notice that the slide has two ends; one end is flat with one opening, while the other is curved with two openings.

- Insert each side of the zipper tape into the curved end at 90° angle. While holding teeth in place, and the zipper tab up as shown, give a gentle push on the slide until the teeth come out the other end of the slide as a closed zipper.

- Slide all the way off and re-install the zipper slide.

- Stop slide in the center, leaving both ends of the zipper tape sealed.

- With right sides together, sew the remaining three sides of the pillow together. Trim the corners and serge the seam allowances. Turn the pillow right side out by opening the zipper. With its nonlocking slide, there is no need to leave an opening in the zipper when sewing it in.

Bag Variations / Corners

BOX CORNERS

Box corners on a bag make for a roomier bag and help it to stand without falling over. The Seven Corner Ruler® has cut-outs to make a variety of box sizes.

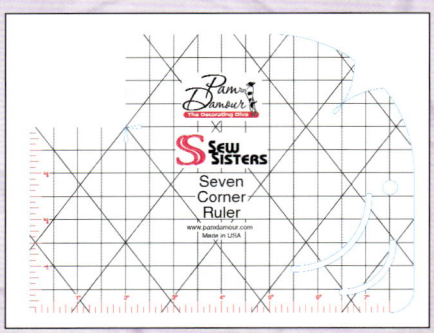

- Sew both the sides and bottom edge of the bag. If the bag bottom does not have a seam, sew side seams.

- Wrap the seams with bias binding.

- If there is a bottom seam and a side seam, fold one seam up and the other down so the seam bulk is more evenly distributed.

- Sew across, back stitching on both ends.

- Bind the corner seam allowance.

Bag Variations / Corners

ROUNDED BOX CORNERS

With our Seven Corner Ruler® you can make corners with soft curves, but still have the fullness of a box corner.

Supplies

- Seven Corner Ruler®
- 28mm Rotary cutter

Construction

- On each bag corner, cut the 3" corner out with your rotary cutter.

- Cut out the center dart.

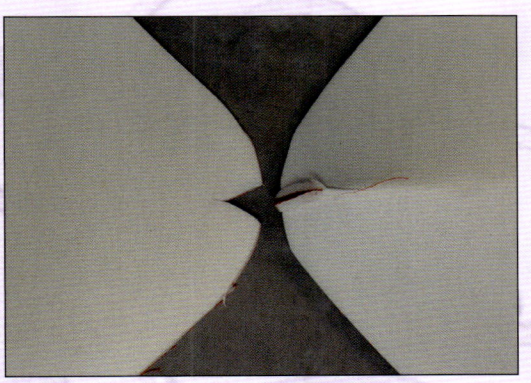

- Sew dart, tapering gradually off the end. Do this on all corners.

- With the dart seams open and lined up, sew the side and bottom seams of bag.

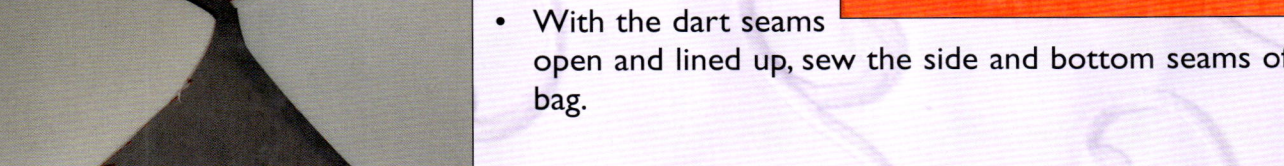

- If making a bag with only side seams and no bottom edge seam, trim like this using your Seven Corner Ruler®. Sew darts, and then side seams all the way around the corner.

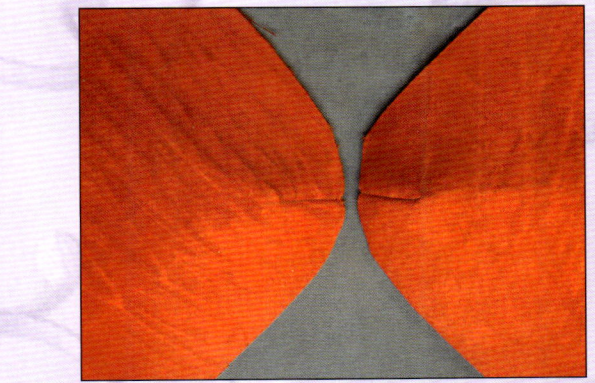

27

Bag Variations / Corners

ROUND CORNERS

There are different ways to make corners on your bags, pockets and other sewing projects. Our Seven Corner Ruler® helps you with making several styles of round corners.

1/2" Curve Corner
- To make the 1/2" curve, use your rotary cutter on the 1/2" curve corner. You can either bind the corner with bias binding or sew a seam.

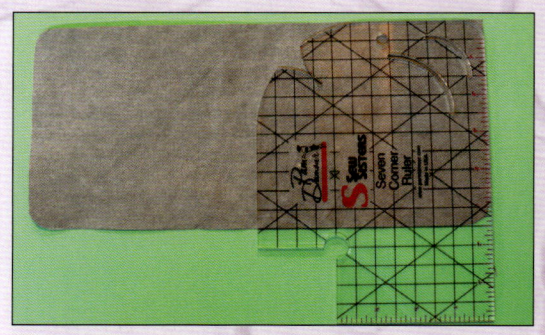

1 1/2" Curve Corner
- Line up the curve by placing the lines on the ruler along the edge of your project. Trace the curve with your FriXion Pen. Cut on the line with scissors, and sew using your preferred method.

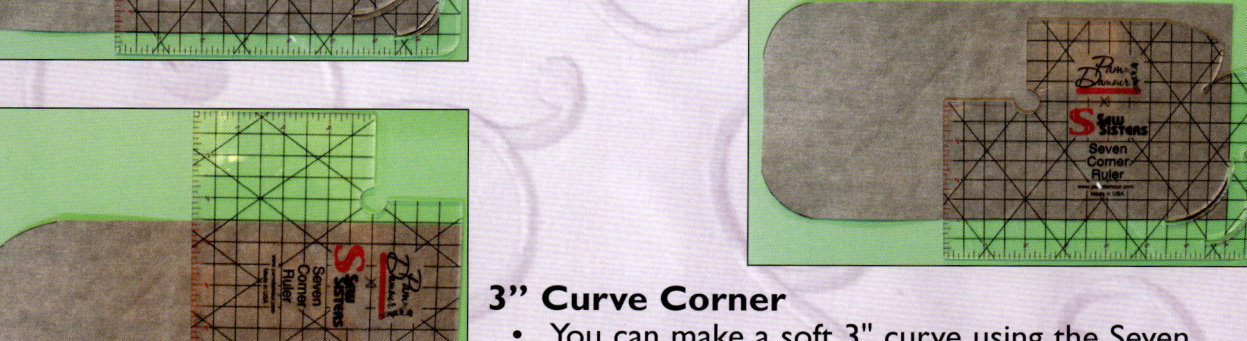

3" Curve Corner
- You can make a soft 3" curve using the Seven Corner Ruler®. You can either trace, and connect your line across the slit, or use your rotary cutter to cut the curve.

2" Curve Corner
- After we developed and named the Seven Corner Ruler®, Betty figured out another corner! Use the 2" corner cut out to mark the top and side of the corner you wish to curve. Align the 3" curve to these marks. Use this part of the 3" curve to draw a line connecting the marks. Cut on the marked line to create your curve.

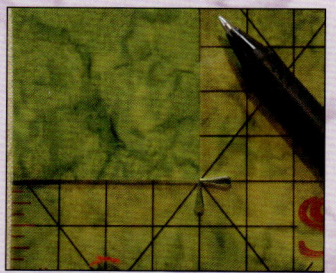 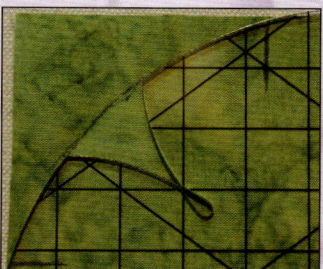  

Bag Variations / Pockets

HANGING ZIPPER POCKET

This is a great flat pocket with a zipper to keep valuables secure. It can be tucked into the top seam of any bag!

Supplies

- Two pocket pieces as per your bag pattern.
- Zipper tape and one slide.
- 2 1/2" bias for sides.

Construction

- Start with your two pocket pieces, one being 1 1/2" longer than the other.

- Sew both ends with a 1/4" seam allowance, RST.

- Since one fabric is cut 1 1/2" longer, the larger side will roll to the back when turned right side out, creating a contrasting flat piping.

- Press seam allowances toward the larger piece.

- Separate your zipper into two pieces and sew each side, with teeth up to the back side of the pocket. Use basting tape to keep zipper in place while sewing.

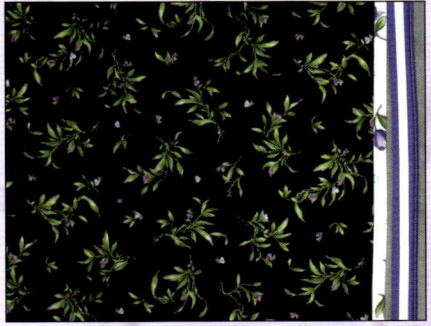

NOTE: I find it most helpful to use a double welting or double piping foot to sew in the zipper. (Names may vary according to brand.)

Bag Variations / Pockets

HANGING ZIPPER POCKET (CONTINUED)

- Insert slide.
- Press pocket flat, with the contrasting flat piping 1 $1/2$" from the top edge.

- Cut two pieces of bias to finish raw edges. Sew onto the wrong side with a $1/2$" seam allowance.
- Fold raw edge under and apply basting tape.

- Bring to the front and stitch along the edge. (See page 47 for more details on sewing binding.)

- Fold bottom ends over, tucking them inside and top stitch in place.
- The top ends of the bias do not need to be finished.

Bag Variations / Pockets

THE HANGING QUILTED POCKET

This pocket has two quilted pieces to cushion your cellphone or anything that needs a little extra protection. By stitching it up the center, you create a double pocket. To stash something larger, leave this step out.

NOTE: *Check your cutting instructions for the bag you're making as sizes do vary from bag to bag.*

Supplies
- Pocket back
- Pocket front
- 2 pieces of Double Sided Fusible Super Shaping Foam®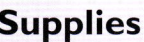
- Bias Binding
- Seven Corner Ruler®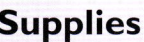
- FriXion Pen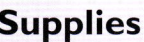
- Edge Joining or Stitch in the Ditch Foot

Construction
- Fold each of your pocket pieces in half with wrong sides together so that they are the same size as the foam. Trim foam if necessary.

- Insert Super Shaping Foam®, bringing foam edge all the way up to the fold.

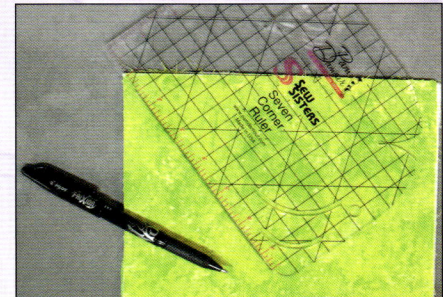

- Fold other side over foam and press to fuse layers together.

- Using the Seven Corner Ruler® (or your favorite quilting ruler), mark quilting lines 1 ½" apart with a FriXion Pen.

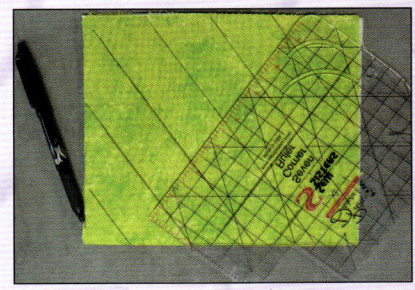

- Quilt both sections by stitching on your lines.

31

Bag Variations / Pockets

THE HANGING QUILTED POCKET (CONTINTUED)

- Using the 1" corner on the Seven Corner Ruler®, cut a curved corner on the bottom (the side opposite the fold) corners.

- Fold the 2" x 8 1/2" strip of contrasting fabric, fold in half lengthwise, wrong sides together and press. (shown in purple)

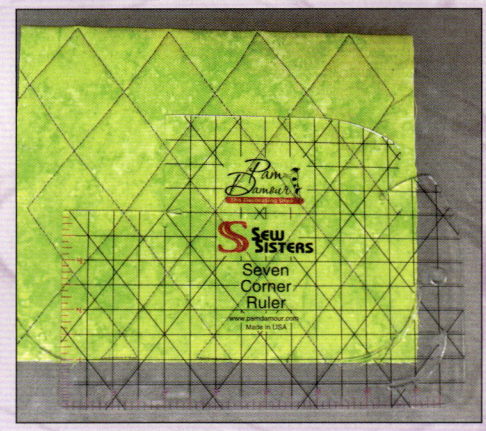

- Sew binding onto the folded edge of the smaller quilted pocket (see page 47 for binding info). Sew on the wrong side of pocket and fold over to the front. Edge stitch folded edge with the Edge Joining or Stitch in the Ditch Foot.

- Pin the smaller pocket section to the larger pocket.

- Mark for center stitching.

- Starting at the bottom, sew along one side of mark, pivot at the top of the small quilted section and sew 2 stitches across the top.

Bag Variations / Pockets

THE HANGING QUILTED POCKET (CONTINUED)

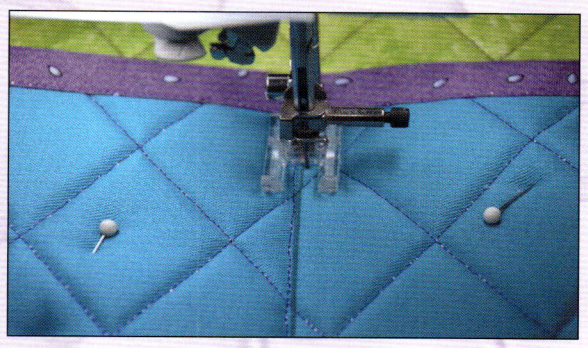

- Sew down on the other side of your mark to the bottom edge.

Quilted Pocket Binding

- Fold your 2 1/2" bias in half lengthwise, with wrong sides together.

- Sew raw edges to one side of the large quilted pocket, with 3/8" seam allowances.

- Roll the folded edge to the right side, pin in place and top stitch in place.

- At the top of the pockets, cut bias off clean and even with the top on both sides.

- When the pocket is sewn into the bag, this will be in the seam allowance so there's no need for finishing the edges.

Bag Variations / Pockets

WIDE CARRY STRAP POCKET

This pocket application is used on the back of the Weekender Bag and the Wheeled Tote.

Supplies
- Pocket cut to size required by pattern. Cut from single sided quilted fabric. Use outside bag fabric.
- Pocket back lining cut to pattern size from lining fabric.
- Welt Cord covered with lining fabric that measures twice the width of the pocket. (See page 55).
- Fabric cut to pattern size for the Buttonhole Zipper Pocket that is added to this pocket. Use lining fabric. (Pocket is longer than it is wide.)

Construction - All seams are 1/2" unless otherwise noted.

- Align Covered Welt Cord to the two long edges of the pocket.

- Using a Welt Cord Foot, stitch Welt Cord in place. (See page 55.)

- Remove 1/2" of cord from each end of the welting. This allows the pocket to stitch flat to the bag.

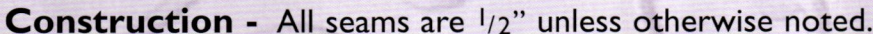

- Use the directions on page 38 to create the Buttonhole Zipper Pocket.

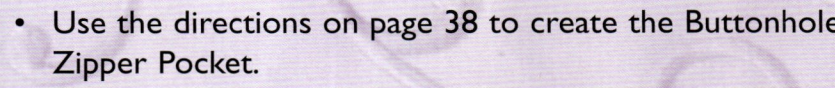

- Start by drawing the zipper box 2" below the top of the fabric, then center the fabric for the Buttonhole Pocket on the Carry Strap Pocket, leaving 1/2" of the pocket fabric above the cut edge of the pocket.

- Continue with the directions on page 38 to complete the pocket.

NOTE: *The opening on the Buttonhole Pocket traditionally features two 'lips' of fabric. This was used on the pocket for the Weekender Bag. For the Wheeled Tote, only a 'hint' of the pocket fabric was allowed to show.*

- With RST and using the Welt Cord Foot, stitch the pocket lining to the pocket along the Welt Cord stitching lines.

Bag Variations / Pockets

WIDE CARRY STRAP POCKET (CONTINUED)

Construction (CONTINUED)
- Turn pocket right side out and press.
- Stitch the bottom of the pocket to the bag back. Use a Welt Cord Foot.

NOTE: For the Wheeled Bag stitch in the ditch between the Welt Cord and the pocket across the full width of the bottom of the pocket. For the Weekender Bag, stitch in the ditch on the bottom of the pocket between the Welt Cord and the pocket for the first 3 1/2" of each side. This leaves an opening in the pocket that can slide over the handle of a rolling suitcase.

- Stitch pocket sides to the sides of the bag.
- Stitch close to the raw edge of the pocket sides.

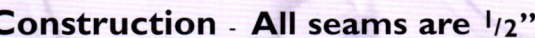

WELT TRIM ZIPPER POCKET

This pocket application is used on the front of the Weekender Bag.

Supplies
- Front pocket is single sided quilted fabric using your outside fabric and cut to pattern size. Fabric may be quilted with Super Shaping Foam® or quilt batting depending on thickness desired.
- Front pocket lining cut to same size as quilted outside front pocket.
- Inside backing – Lining fabric cut to pocket width and 1/2" shorter than outside quilted piece.
- Front pocket band/backing – Coordinating fabric cut to width of the outside and 2" longer. This is the piece that creates the band on the pocket top.
- Welt Cord covered with accent fabric that measures twice the width of the pocket.
- Zipper tape measuring the width of the pocket.
- One zipper slide.

Construction - All seams are 1/2"

NOTE: There are three layers to this pocket construction – Outside, Inside and Finishing.

- Mark a horizontal line 1 1/2" below the top edge of the quilted outside piece.

Bag Variations / Pockets

WELT TRIM ZIPPER POCKET (CONTINUED)

Construction (CONTINUED)

- Cut the outside along this line.
- Cut the covered Welt Cord in half and stitch a piece to each cut edges created when you cut the outside pocket into 2 pieces.
- Press seams to the inside.
- Align the zipper teeth with the edge of the Welt Cord.
- Stitch Welt Cord to the top and bottom of the outside pocket pieces by stitching in the ditch along the welt/pocket seams.

- If you wish to monogram your pocket this is the time to do that. Center monogram in the lower portion of the outside pocket.
- Cut the front pocket lining into two pieces as you did the outside pocket.
- Stitch the right side of each pieces of fabric to the wrong side of the zipper tape and press.
- This will create the finished look for the back of the front pocket.

- Remove 1/2" of Welt Cord from each side of each piece. This will make it easier to stitch the side seams with less bulk.
- Insert zipper pull.
- Place the outside pocket front on top of the inside backing piece - the back side of the pocket front should be RST with the inside backing piece.
- Stitch around top and side edges with a 1/4" seam.
- Front Pocket Band/Backing – turn under top edge 1/2" and press.
- Align pressed edge with the top piece of welt and top stitch along the folded edge.

- Wrap remaining fabric to the back, pressing along the top edge.
- Stitch sides together with 1/4" seam.
- Trim bottom edges even, matching to the shortest piece.
- Stitch bottom edges with a 1/4" seam.

Bag Variations / Pockets

POCKET WITH WELT TRIM AND ACCENT BAND

This pocket application is used on the sides of the Weekender Bag and the Wheeled Tote.

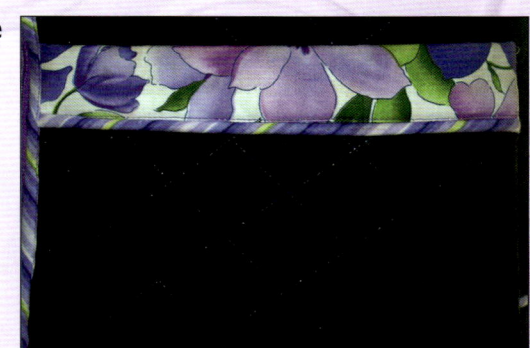

Supplies
- Pocket cut to required size from double sided quilted fabric.
- Covered Welt Cord that measures width of the pocket. (See page 55.)
- Fabric for accent band that measures width of the pocket by 4" high.

Construction All seams are 1/2" unless otherwise noted.

- Measure 1" from the top edge of the pocket front and align cut edge of Welt Cord to this line.

- Using a Welt Cord Foot, stitch Welt Cord in place.

- Remove 1/2" of cord from each end of the welting. This allows the pocket to stitch flat to the bag.

- Measure 1" from top edge on pocket back and mark a line.

- Align cut edge of accent band to the marked line.

- Stitch band to back using a 1/2" seam. Use a Welt Cord Foot – you will be stitching through the stitching line used to attach the cord on the front.

- Press accent band toward pocket top.

- Press band over the edge, pressing cut edge under 1/2" and aligning fold with the edge of the Welt Cord.

- Topstitch close to the pressed edge.

Bag Variations / Pockets

BUTTONHOLE ZIPPER POCKET

Similar to our Buttonhole Zipper Insertion, with this technique, the buttonhole opening is also the pocket, because the placket fabric is cut large enough to fold up and create the pocket. (See Buttonhole Zipper Insertion on page 21 for more detailed instructions.)

Supplies
- Placket/pocket fabric
- FriXion Pen
- Zipper tape with 1 slide
- Peel & stick or Décor Bond stabilizer

Construction
- On the pocket fabric, draw your zipper box in the location specified by your pattern. Draw a line down the center with a "Y" at each end.

- Sew zipper box on the line starting on one of the long sides.

- Cut on each side of the center line. This will leave a thin amount of fabric in the center. Cut this away.

- Pull the pocket fabric through the opening to the back. Allow the pocket fabric to wrap around the Shaping Foam to create a "piping".

- Press the pocket opening. With basting tape on each side of the zipper, place the zipper on the back of the opening.

- Stitch in the ditch all the way around the zipper box.

Bag Variations / Pockets

BUTTONHOLE ZIPPER POCKET (CONTINUED)

Construction (CONTINUED)

- Trim off excess zipper tape, leaving 1/2" at each end.
- Fold the pocket in half, bringing the bottom edge even with the top.
- Sew the sides and top edges of pocket.

Open Buttonhole Zipper Pocket

- This application has a larger opening and can be made with or without a zipper.
- On the top end of the wrong side of your Zipper Pocket, draw a 1/2" by 5 1/2" box, 1 1/2" down from the top edge, centering on the pocket.
- Draw a line down the center, making a "Y" at each end.

- With right sides together, pin the pocket top 1 1/2" from the top edge of the bag lining, centering it.
- Sew all the way around the box, starting along one of the long sides. Do not sew past the corner and do not back stitch. If you do, rip it out and start over.
- Cut down the middle of the box all the way into the "Y" at the corners.
- Pull all the pocket fabric to the back and press flat.
- Install zipper slide on your zipper tape, leaving both ends closed.
- Use basting tape or pins to position the zipper to the back of the pocket opening.
- Top stitch all the way around your zipper box opening to secure zipper.
- Trim zipper ends if they extend more than a 1/2" from the end of the zipper box.

Bag Variations / Pockets

THE DIVIDING ZIPPER POCKET

This inserted pocket is great for dividing your bag into different compartments. The inner stabilizer keeps the pocket's shape so that it can hold file folders, laptop or tablet.

Supplies
- Face fabric
- Lining fabric
- Stabilizer
- Zipper
- Zipper slides

Construction

- Cut your pocket front, back, stabilizer and zipper according to your pattern's directions.

- Fuse the stabilizer to the wrong side of the face fabric. Stabilizer should go all the way to the side edges, but be 1/2" shorter at the top and bottom.

- Separate your zipper into two pieces and with RST, sew each side of the zipper to the two top edges of the pocket face fabric.

- With right sides together, sew the lining to the face fabric along the zippered edges, sandwiching the zipper in between the two layers of fabric. (The sides are still open)

- Turn right side out and press, exposing the zipper teeth. Install your zipper slide at one end, or at both ends if making a two-way zipper. (See page 23.)

- Press flat with the zipper at the top edge.

- Serge or zig zag the sides.

NOTE: Since this pocket is being inserted into a seam at each side of your bag, a serged or zig-zag finish is fine.

Bag Variations / Pockets

EASY BINDING POCKET

This Easy Binding technique has multiple applications. We used it here on pockets for Jaclyn's Bag and the Wheeled Tote.

Supplies

- Pocket and pocket lining cut to size per pattern directions.

NOTE: *The pocket lining is always 1" longer than the pocket.*

- Some form of interfacing or stabilization will help the pocket to retain its proper shape. Pocket piece may be interfaced, interlined, backed with batting or foam, quilted, etc., depending on the requirements of the specific pattern.

Construction

- With RST, stitch together the top edges of the pocket and the pocket lining with a scant ½" seam allowance.

- Press the seam allowance toward the pocket lining. (This is the longer of the two pieces.)

- Press pocket lining over the cut edge of the seam allowance encasing it to create the Easy Binding.

- Top stitch close to the lower edge of the binding or stitch in the ditch along the seam line.

- Stitch together close to the side and bottom edges of the pocket.

Bag Variations / Straps

ADJUSTABLE STRAP

Adjustable straps are great when you want to go from a shoulder bag to a cross-over bag. The measurements in this book are merely a guideline. You may want to measure for your desired length before cutting.

If you are going to make an adjustable strap, you will need to use some hardware. You will need a slider on the strap and a square or D-ring. You will also need a strap end piece. Some like to add a strap clip so the strap can be removed. Some like hardware on both sides. This is all personal preference. This method works with pre-made strapping or a strap you make yourself.

Supplies

- Bag strap
- 1 (or 2) bag strap ends
- Strap slider
- D-ring or square ring

Construction

- Construct strap according to your project directions.

- Assemble your strap by pulling through the slider, through the D-ring and back though the slider.

- Fold the finished end over the center of the slider and stitch in place.

Bag Strap End

- Pull finished end through D-ring, fold over and sew down along edge.

Optional: You may want to add a D-ring Bag Strap end to each end of your bag.

Bag Variations / Straps

PIPED STRAP

This bag strap has piping on each side, with Deco-Magic® or Kraft•Tex™ in the center, creating a firm strap able to support a heavy bag.

Supplies
- Deco-Magic® cut 1" wide by the length of your strap
- Piping or zipper foot
- Bias cut fabric for back of strap and piping 2 1/2" wide by the length of your strap
- Fabric for the front side of strap cut 1 1/2" wide by the length of the strap
- Micro Welt Cord (Twice the length of your strap.)
- Basting tape

Construction
- Cut straps to desired width and length. If making a continuous one-piece strap like the one on the Teacher's Pet Bag, piece the strap fabric with diagonal seams so the bulk is not all in one place.

- Sew both fabrics RST with a 1/2" seam allowance.

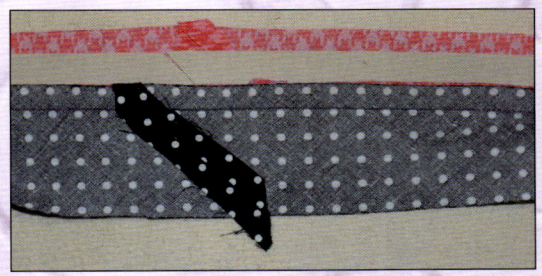

- Press fusible side of the Deco-Magic® strip to the wrong side of front strap fabric. Line Micro Welt Cord up to the edge of the stitching.

- Tuck the piping inside so that the back fabric wraps around the cord and the needle is stitching in the ditch between the two fabrics. Leave some cord free at the beginning for splicing.

- Press the excess seam allowance over the edge of the Deco-Magic®.

- Place basting tape along the edge of the fold where the piping will be placed.

Bag Variations / Straps

PIPED STRAP (CONTINUED)

- Place Micro Welt Cord on the basting tape and fold remaining side under the top (pink) fabric, wrapping the Micro Welt Cord.

- To make the other side, stitch on the edge of the front fabric (pink fabric).

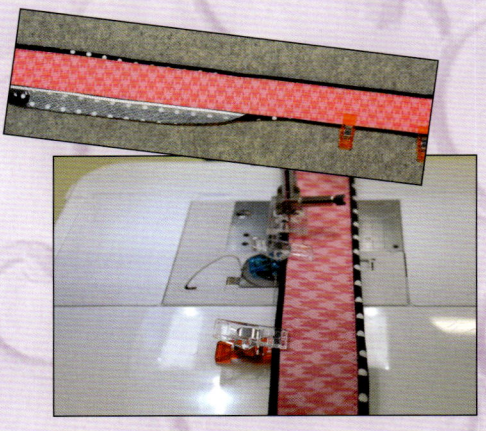

- If you have to join the cord, cut both cord ends at an angle to match each other and tuck ends inside to complete the piping.

Kraft•Tex™ Piped Strap

The beauty of using Kraft-Tex™ in your handbag project is that it looks and feels like leather, but it is washable and easier to sew than leather. It is actually a paper product, but you can't tear it, nor does it stretch like leather does.

Supplies

- Kraft•Tex™ cut 1" wide (or desired width)
- Bias cut fabric strip, cut 2 1/2" wide (or 1 1/2" wider than the Kraft•Tex™)
- Micro Welt Cord (Twice the length of your strap)
- Basting tape

Construction

- Fold fabric over 1/2" and pin or Wonder Clip the Micro Welt Cord into fold.

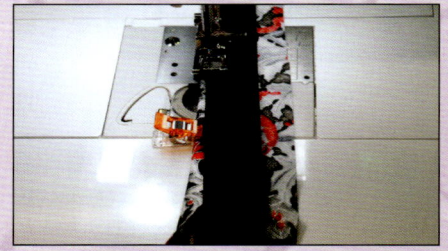

- Butt the Kraft•Tex™ up to the cord and stitch along the edge of Kraft•Tex™, making a corded edge as you sew. You may need to adjust your needle position.

- Place basting tape along the other edge of the Kraft•Tex™ where your Micro Welt Cord will be.

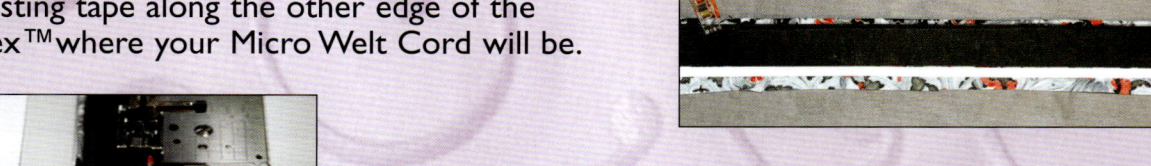

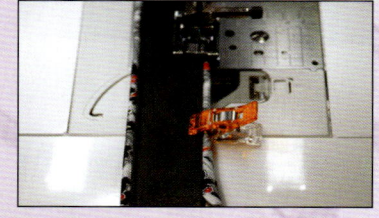

- Wrap bias over the Micro Welt Cord. The basting tape will hold it in place. Wonder Clip in place, and stitch on the other edge of Kraft•Tex™.

Bag Variations / Straps

PADDED STRAP

There are times when you may want a softer padded strap for your bag. To make this, cut your fabric 2 x the finished width, plus 1 $\frac{1}{4}$", and add 2" to the finished length.

Supplies

- Strap fabric cut to size according to your pattern.
- Super Shaping Foam® cut to size according to your pattern.
- Press Perfect Iron Finger
- Fast Turn Tube Turner to fit the size of your strap

- Cut Super Shaping Foam® the finished length x the finished width.

- Sew a tube, with $\frac{1}{2}$" seam allowances.

- Press seam open with the Press Perfect Iron Finger Tool.

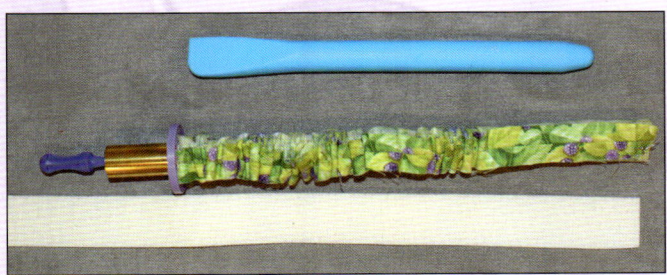

- Slide fabric onto the appropriate size Fasturn Tube Turner.

- Use the accompanying insert to secure the fabric by twisting the handle. (I usually twist it through the fabric twice to secure it.)

- Stuff the Super Shaping Foam® in the end of the tube before pulling through the tube turner.

- As you pull the fabric through, the foam will come with it, like magic! There's no need to hook it!

Bag Variations / Straps

DOUBLE FOLDED PADDED STRAP

Straps are cut 4 times the desired finished width. Cut as many strips as you need for the required length.

Construction

- Cut the strips the desired width by WOF, cutting enough strips to achieve the required length. You will need to cut 10"-15" extra to insure you have enough length to seam the strips together.

- Join the strap sections with bias seams.

- From the remaining Super Shaping Foam®, cut 2 strips that measure 1/4 the finished strap width by the 58" length of the foam.

NOTE: If you want extra padding cut the foam a scant 2 times the finished width of the strap. This will give you a double layer of padding in the strap.

- Press the strap fabric piece in half lengthwise.

- Open and press each side toward the center.

- Open and lay the strips of foam between the center crease and one of the side creases.

- Fuse the foam in place.

- Fold and press again.

- Topstitch both sides of the strap piece close to the outside edges and set aside.

NOTE: Topstitching is much easier if you stitch close to the fold before stitching the open edges together.

Great Finishes / Binding

BIAS BINDING

Bias binding is a great way to finish seams and edges adding minimum bulk. While many choose to cut their strips on the straight of grain, my preference has always been to cut my strips on the bias, especially when there are curved edges.

NOTE: Sometimes I sew my binding on the right side and wrap to the back. Sometimes I sew it on the back and wrap to the front. It all depends on the project!

- Start by sewing with a 1/2" seam allowance. As you approach a corner, fold your binding fabric at a 45° angle and press a crease with your finger nail.

- Unfold fabric and if necessary, mark crease with a fabric marker.

- Sew to your crease or mark and backstitch to secure. Do not sew past your mark.

- Cut thread and remove from machine.

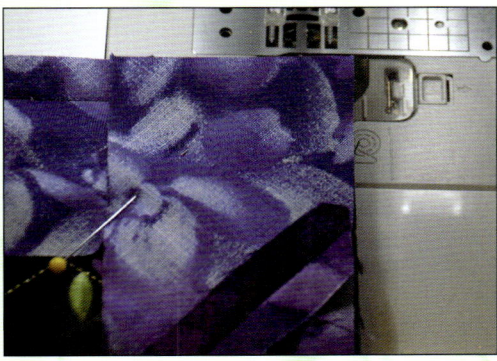

- Pivot project 90° and refold binding at previous place.

- Fold binding back over with right sides together, with the top edge of binding even with the edge of your project.

47

Great Finishes / Binding

BIAS BINDING (CONTINUED)

- Begin sewing at the top edge. If sewing around the edge of another pocket or edge, you may need to switch to a Narrow Zipper Foot.

- Tuck the raw edge under, fold over, and use basting tape to keep in place.

- Fold over binding so that the fold just covers the previous stitching line.

- Pin in place, mitering corners and hand stitch or top stitch in place.

- When sewing binding on the top edge of a bag, finish by folding the top layer over 1/2" at the beginning at an angle.

- Cut the end at the same angle, overlapping about 1".

- Wrap both edges together with the folded edge on top. Use basting tape to hold the folded edge in place before sewing.

Great Finishes / Binding

FRENCH BINDING

French Binding is similar to regular binding, but you first fold the binding fabric in half with wrong sides together. Because it has a double thickness, it will wear better. Use this binding on edges that will see lots of wear.

- Sew a scant one third seam allowance of the width of the folded binding.

NOTE: *Sew a small test sample to make sure your binding will wrap the project in the correct place.*

- Fold the binding end over at a 45° angle, finger crease and sew to the crease line.

- Fold end back over even with the open edge of project and sew down.

- Fold over to the other side and pin in place. Top stitch down in place.

- When sewing a curved binding, it is imperative that you cut your binding fabric on the bias. (See page 10 for Bias.)

- Fold binding in half RST and press. Sew with raw edges together, with a third scant seam allowance, as you would for French Binding.

- As you sew the curve, ease the binding into the curve without stretching.

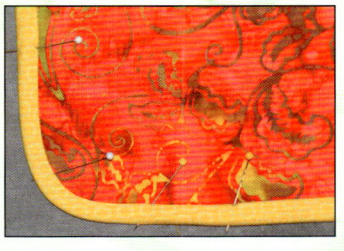

- Wrap the folded edge over, pin in place and top stitch.

Great Finishes

MACHINE QUILTING WITH THE SEVEN CORNER RULER®

You can use any of your quilting rulers for marking quilting lines. On our Seven Corner Ruler®, we've marked out lines that give a gentle diamond pattern. It is more pointed than making 45° angles, but less pointed than using your 60/30 lines.

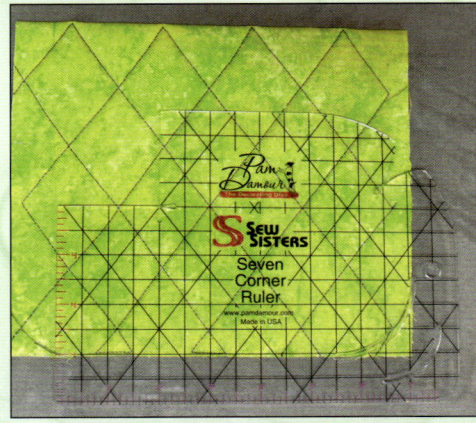

Construction

- Fuse your fabric with Super Shaping Foam®.

- Mark lines for quilting using a FriXion Pen.
  (I usually mark my lines 1 1/2" apart.)

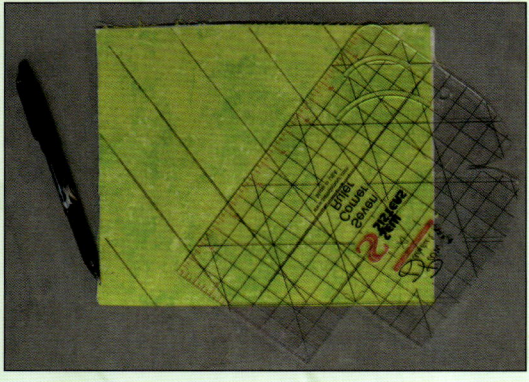

- Mark in two directions to achieve the diamond pattern, but parallel lines are fine too!

- Machine quilt with your favorite thread!
  (I used Lamé Stylo.)

Great Finishes

FRENCH SEAMS

French Seams are hundreds of years old and were popular in clothing construction before the invention of sergers or zig-zag sewing machines. French seams provide a clean finish because all the seam allowances are encased in the seam.

French seams are not generally used on curves due to the bulk they create.

Construction

- Sew fabric layers with wrong sides together with a 1/4" seam allowance.

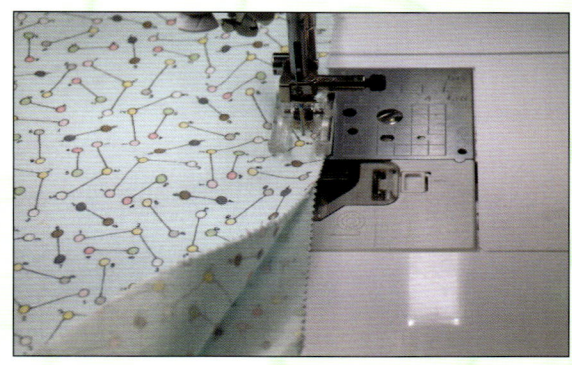

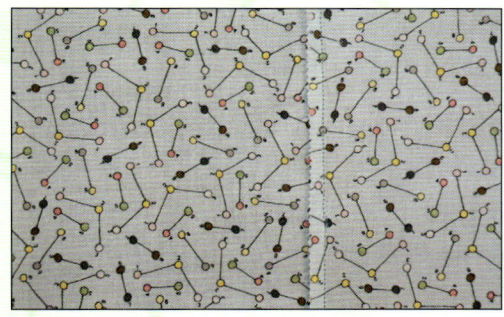

- Trim seam close, about 1/8", with plain or pinking shears.

- Press to one side.

- With right sides together, and previous seam along the edge, stitched seam to the edge, sew a seam with 1/4" seam allowance, encasing the raw edges of the previous seam.

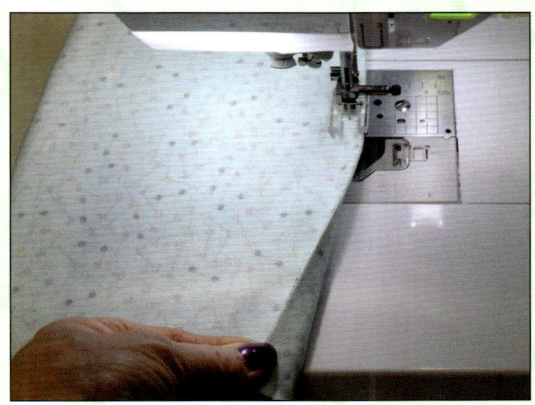

- Press finished seam to one side.

Great Finishes

LAMINATING FABRIC

Laminating your own fabric is fun and easy. This allows you to make your own waterproof fabrics, great to be used on lunch bags, make-up bags, rain coats and more!

For this book, we used an Iron-on, sewable vinyl, and a brush on fabric coating gel.

Supplies
- Fabric prewashed and free of sizing and fabric softener
- Iron-on laminating vinyl
- Good quality iron
- Optional: Magic Pressing Mat, lint roller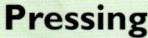

Construction
- Press fabric flat, and remove any excess fiber, fuzz and or threads. (I use the lint roller here.)

- Cut laminating sheet to size and remove the backing paper.
- Apply vinyl, tacky side down to the right side of your fabric.

Pressing
- Use the backing paper you pulled off to press your vinyl. With shiny side down against the vinyl, press (Do not iron!), starting from the center out and holding your iron in place at least 8 seconds.

CAUTION! Don not let your iron touch the vinyl directly!
- I save my larger pieces of backing paper for future laminating, or use a teflon laminating sheet.
- Allow fabric to cool, and peel off pressing sheet.
- Sew as you would normal fabric. If you find the fabric sticks to the presser foot, use a Teflon foot.

HELPFUL HINT: *If you have trouble with your presser foot sticking to the laminated fabric, use either a roller foot or Teflon foot to help fabric glide a bit better. Always press laminated fabric from the wrong side. Test your fabric.*

Great Finishes

BRUSH ON FABRIC COATING GEL

Odicoat® Gel is a great alternative to the Iron-on Vinyl, albeit a little more work. You can brush on one, two or three coats to achieve the desired effect. While a little more time consuming and mess than the iron-on counter part, it is more pliable and softer to the hand.

Supplies
- Odicoat® Fabric Coating Gel
- Paint brush
- Fabric to be laminated
- Surface to put fabric on, (I use the back of a cutting mat, but you could use a plastic table cloth, and/or newspaper.)

Construction

- Prewash fabric to remove any sizing.

- Lay your fabric with wrong side up and brush the Odicoat® Gel evenly on the wrong side.

- Let dry thoroughly and repeat with one or two coats, depending on desired effect.

- Sew as you would normal fabric. If you find the fabric sticks to the presser foot, use a Teflon foot.

Odicoat is a product of Odif USA. Here are some other products we love from Odif USA.

53

Great Finishes / Finishing Techniques

ZIPPER AND SEAM TRIM

This trim will give your bag a real custom look. Additionally, it has a very practical application for helping to eliminate some of the bulk in seams when using heavier batting or foam to stabilize your bags.

Supplies

- 2" wide bias strips measuring the length required by the pattern.
- Accent or matching thread for topstitching the trim fabric.
- Thread to match the zipper being used.

Construction

- Press bias strip in half lengthwise.
- Align raw edges of the trim with the edge of the bag indicated in pattern directions.
- Serge or zigzag stitch the raw edges of the bag and the trim together.
- Topstitch close to the folded edge of the trim.

- With a zipper trim application, once the trim has been applied, stitch each side of the zipper to the trim RST following the general zipper instructions on page 25. Make sure the top thread matches the zipper tape.

- Press the zipper tape open on the inside.

- Topstitch both sides of the trim close to the pressed fold near the zipper.

NOTE: If this is an application to embellish a seam, the trim will be applied after the pockets have been placed on the bag. The top stitching will then serve to stitch the pockets in place. As a result, the trim, not the thicker pocket fabric, will be caught in the seam allowance. Once the trim has been applied, the seams will be stitched as usual. When applying trim to a curve, be sure to ease the trim around the curve, stretching a little so that the folded edge of the trim lies flat on the fabric.

Great Finishes / Finishing Techniques

WELT CORD

Welt cord or piping, comes in many sizes. The standard in home decorating is about 1/4" across. Micro Welt is about 1/8" across and Jumbo Welt is about 1/2" across. Welt cord is the perfect trim when you want to add an accent, a bit of color or stabilize an edge.

Foot Required

Depending on which foot you have, use either the 1/4" Welt Cord Foot, the Piping Foot or a Zipper Foot.

Other Requirements

- Standard Welt Cord or Micro Welt Cord
- For 1/8" Micro Welt Cord, cut bias 1 1/2"
- For 1/4" Welt Cord, cut bias 2"
- 5-in-1 Ruler®

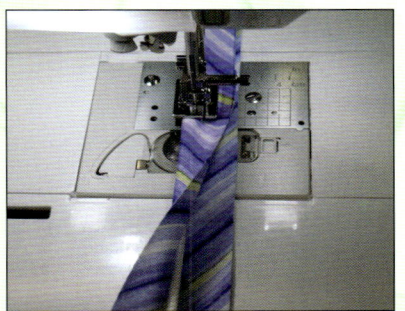

Construction

- Fold bias strip over welt cord and place under presser foot with the cord under the deep groove of the welt cord foot.

- If your foot has a left groove, use a center needle position with a stitch length of 3.0 and move needle 2 positions to the right.

- If your foot has a center groove, move your needle all the way to the right.

- Or, if you don't own a machine with a 1/4" Welt Cord Foot, use your zipper foot and move the needle all the way over to the left, lining up with the edge of the foot.

- Trim after sewing using the Pam Damour 5-in-1 Ruler® to get an accurate 1/2" seam allowance.

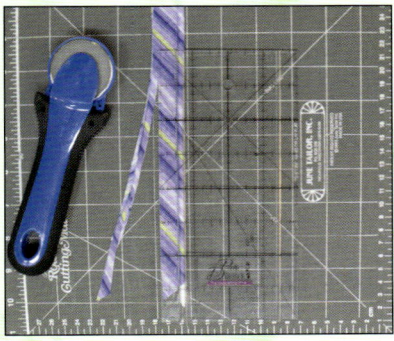

Sewing Welt or Piping onto Fabric

- Using welt cord already made, move one needle position to the right.
- Match raw edges of welt with the edge of fabric. Sew welt cord onto fabric, stitching between the original stitching line and the cord.

Great Finishes / Finishing Techniques

WELT CORD (CONTINUED)

Corners

- To turn the corner, make three snips, all the way to the stitching line. The center snip should be at $1/2$" from the edge of the project. (See arrow.)
- Turn the corner, and using your stiletto, push the fabric back into the corner.
- Sew into place.
- Repeat this for the remaining three corners.

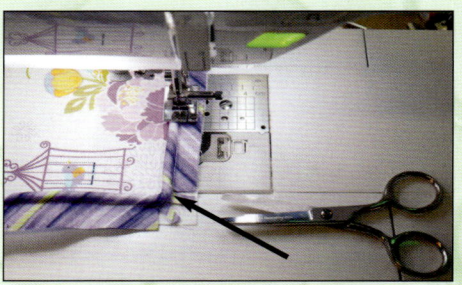

Splicing the Cord

- To join the cord, sew all the way around leaving about a 2" space from where the cord started.
- Trim the ending end straight across, with about a 3" overlap.
- Trim the starting end at a 45° angle.
- Rip the welt stitching as shown and trim the welt cord at the same 45° angle as the beginning end.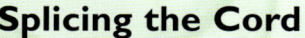
- Fold the unstitched fabric over, wrong sides together, at a 45° angle at the beginning end.
- Angle as shown.
- Fold over and sew in place, holding everything together with a stiletto.

Micro Welt

- When making micro welt use a foot with a smaller groove or a zipper foot. Use the small groove in the 5-in-1 Ruler®. Turn corners and splice as you would with the standard cord.

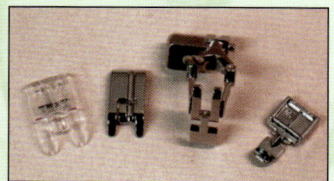

Organizers

Organizers

THE HOLD EVERYTHING BAG!

This bag is a simple bag with some key features. You can make it as simple or as complicated as you prefer. It has a large padded pocket to hold your tablet, cell phone or anything else you might want to conceal. Inside there are pockets on each side of the bag and a key fob. All fabrics used here are quilting weight cottons.

Supplies

- Main fabric: 1 1/4 yards
- Lining: 7/8 yard
- Accent fabric: 1/2 yard
- FriXion Pen and/or Magic Chalk
- Seven Corner Ruler ®
- Lamé Stylo decorative thread
- 45" of zipper tape and 5 slides
- 2 of 1 1/4" D-rings; 2 of 1 1/4" swivel clips; 1 of 1 1/4" adjustable strap slider
- 1/4" Basting tape
- Small swivel clip for key fob
- 7 1/2" Quick Clutch Wallet Clasp
- Hot glue gun
- Flat Head Screwdriver
- Size 00 Phillips Head Screwdriver
- Bonash Fusing Powder and pressing sheet
- Double welting foot
- Narrow zipper foot
- Super Shaping Foam ® Double Side Fusible: Small size (18" x 58")
- Deco-Magic®: 1 - 7 1/2" x 10 1/2"; 1 - 52" x 1 1/4", 1 - 10 1/2" x 10"
- Peel & Stick stabilizer for wallet: 3 - 2" by 7 1/2"; 1 - 3 1/2" x 7 1/2"; 1 - 5" x 7 1/2"

Fabric provided by Maywood Studios, Catalina Ultra Violet Collection

Organizers

THE HOLD EVERYTHING BAG! (CONTINUED)

Cutting

Main Fabric
- Bag body: 2 - 11" x 14"
- Outside pocket: 1 - 11" x 9"; and 1 - 11" x 10 1/2"
- Hanging zipper pocket: 1 - 15 1/2" x 9"
- Inner quilted pocket: 1 - 9" x 14"
- Pocket vent: 1 - 3 1/2" x 11"
- Bag strap ends: 2 - 3 1/2" x 6"
- Bag strap: 1 - 3 1/2" x 42"

Wallet Parts Cut From Main Fabric
- Wallet outside: 1 - 8 1/2" x 10 1/2"
- Wallet zipper pocket: 2 - 8 1/2" x 9 1/2"
- Wallet card pocket: 1 - 4" x 8 1/2"
- Wallet top pocket: 1 - 7" x 8 1/2"

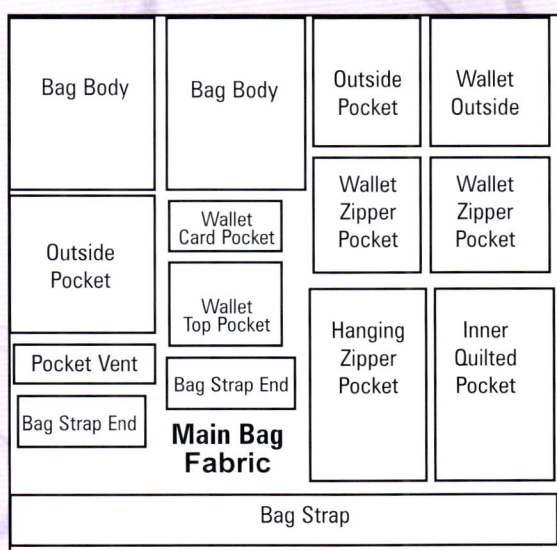

Lining Fabric
- Bag body inside: 2 - 11" x 14"
- Outside pocket: 1 - 11" x 9"; and 1 - 11" x 10 1/2"
- Hanging zipper pocket: 1 - 14" x 9"
- Double quilted pocket: 1 - 9" x 10"

Wallet Parts From Lining Fabric
- Wallet inside: 1 - 8 1/2" x 12"
- Card pocket: 1 - 4" x 8 1/2"
- Zipper placket: 1 - 2 1/2" x 8 1/2"

Accent Fabric: 1/2 yard
- Top zipper placket: 2 - 4" x 12"
- Zipper tabs 2 - 2" x 2"
- 3 1/2" yards of 2 1/2" bias
- 1 - 2" x 6" for Key Fob

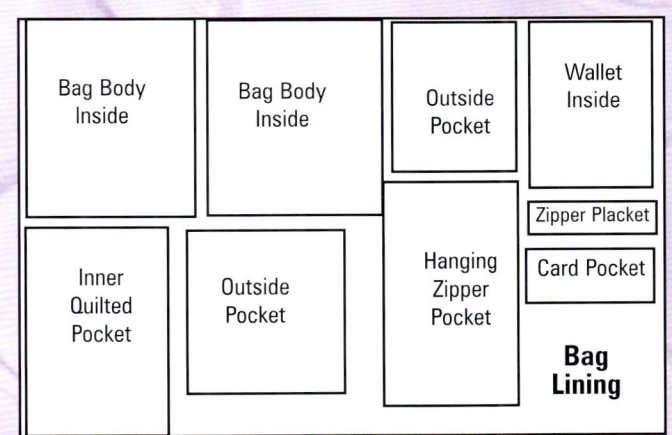

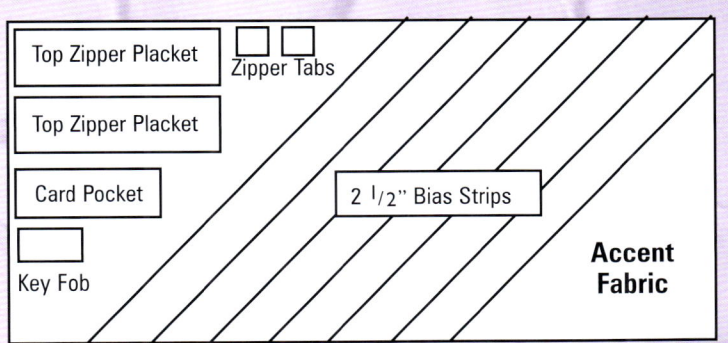

59

Organizers

THE HOLD EVERYTHING BAG! (CONTINUED)

Cutting (CONTINUED)

Wallet Parts Cut from Accent Fabric
- Card pocket: 1 - 4" x 8 1/2"

Stabilizer
- Super Shaping Foam® Double Side Fusible:
  2 - 11" x 14"; 1 - 9" x 7";
  1 - 9" x 5"; & 1 - 11" x 9"

| Bag Body 11" x 14" | Bag Body 11" x 14" | Outside Pocket 11" x 9" | Inner Quilted Pocket 9" x 7" | Inner Quilted Pocket 9" x 5" |

Super Shaping Foam

Construction
- With the main fabric bag body and lining fabric bag body pieces, use the double-sided Super Shaping Foam® to make two "fabric sandwiches".

- Press to fuse all three layers together. Mark for quilting lines with your FriXion Pen or Magic Chalk using the Seven Corner Ruler® (or your favorite ruler for marking) with lines 1 1/2" apart.

- (See page 50 for more on marking and quilting.)

- Stitch on your lines.

- Using the Seven Corner Ruler®, or your favorite ruler, cut out a 1" square at each of the bottom corners. (We chose to show this with the bag lining so you can see the ruler and cut better.)

IMPORTANT NOTE: After making a few of these bags, I found it tricky to finish the top binding with the wallet attached to the bag, so I had to rethink the assembly. Start by sewing the side seams down just enough so that the top zipper plackets, inside pockets and binding can be sewn on before the outer pockets.

Organizers

THE HOLD EVERYTHING BAG! (CONTINUED)
Construction (CONTINUED)

- After both bottom corners are cut, put bag sides together and starting from the top, sew side seams down 2 1/2", with a 1/2" seam allowance.

- Cut two 10" pieces of 2 1/2" binding, and sew down 2" starting at the top edge of each side seam.

- Roll your bias to the other side of the seam, folding the raw edge under. Starting at the top, sew along the folded edge 1". (See binding on page 47.)

The Hanging Pockets

- This bag has two inner pockets. See page 31 for the Hanging Quilted Pocket and page 29 for Hanging Zipper Pocket.

- Pin one pocket to the top edge of each of the lining sides of the bag.

- If you wish to include a key fob to the inside of the bag, go to page 15 for directions, and pin fob in place inside the top edge of the bag near one end.

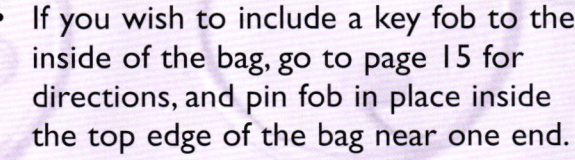

- Cut your zipper tape 16". Make the two-way top zipper placket and pin to the top edge of bag. (See page 23.)

- Sew top edge with a 3/8" seam allowance, attaching the inner pockets and the top zipper placket.

61

Organizers

THE HOLD EVERYTHING BAG! (CONTINUED)
The Strap

- Cut your Deco-Magic® 1 1/4" wide, and your strap fabric 3 3/4" wide. (I have also used Kraft•Tex™ with the Bonash Powder for the inside of the strap and it works great!)

NOTE: *This measurement is for strap hardware with a 1 1/4" inside opening. Please check your hardware and adjust your strap width to fit your hardware.*

- Fuse the Deco-Magic® to the wrong side of the fabric, lining up along one edge.

- Press other edge under 1/2".

- Wrap fabric around Deco-Magic® strap.

- Topstitch on both edges.

- Turn to page 42 and follow the instructions to make an adjustable strap.

- Sew strap centered over the seam about 1" below top edge of the bag, with ends turned under.

- Make strap ends in the same manner, trimming Deco-Magic® so that it is 1/2" shorter at the ends.

- Pin the strap tabs on the top edge of bag, with the raw edges lined up to the top edge of the bag, centered over the side seams.

Organizers

THE HOLD EVERYTHING BAG! (CONTINUED)

Top Binding

After you pin the Strap Tabs, Hanging Inner Pockets, Key Fob and Two Way Zipper Placket pieces to the bag top edge, it's time to add your binding!

- Fold the beginning end of your binding fabric under 1/2" at a 45° angle and press flat.

- Add bias binding to the inside of the top edge to cover all the raw edges, using a scant 1/2" seam allowance.

HELPFUL HINT: *If your sewing machine has a free arm, it will make sewing the binding much easier, as you can slip the bag over the free arm.*

- When sewing over the top seams, fold one side up and the other down as you sew across them. This will make them face in the same direction inside the bag and will make the corners easier.

- Apply basting tape just below your stitching line on your bag.

- Wrap the bias from back to front, turning about 1/2" under. Fold your end edge under 1/2" or so.

- Fold bias over basting tape and secure before top stitching along the folded edge. The tape will keep your bias from stretching as you sew.

The Attached Wallet

This bag has an attached wallet on one side. You can choose to omit this, make the wallet to be used inside or attached as shown on this bag.

Wallet Modifications

NOTE: Please refer to page 92 for detailed Quick Clutch Wallet directions. The modifications for this wallet are included with these instructions.

Organizers

THE HOLD EVERYTHING BAG! (CONTINUED)
Wallet Modifications (CONTINUED)

- This wallet is made with the Deco-Magic® in place of the Super Shaping Foam®. Your padding or stiffener in your wallet is a personal choice, so feel free to be creative. This wallet outside is not quilted.

- Fuse Deco-Magic® to the wrong side of the wallet outside. Set aside.

Wallet Inside

- Stabilize and sew pocket assembly. (See page 93 for more detailed instructions.)

Wallet Zipper Pocket

- Layer two zipper pocket fabrics with wrong sides together.

- Draw the zipper box: 1/2" wide by 5 1/2" long and centered on the wrong side of the zipper placket.

- With right sides together, place your zipper placket on your zipper pocket fabric.

- The top edge of the placket needs to be 2 3/4" from the top edge of the pocket.

- Sew your zipper box, starting along one of the long sides.

- Do not sew outside of the box. If you do, do not back stitch. RIP IT OUT! I mean it! Wink Wink.

- You will not get a smooth zipper opening if you back stitch. Count your stitches at each end to keep the sides even.

- Cut down the middle, and to the corners making a "Y". (See page 38.)

- Pull placket fabric through the opening to the back and pleat ends as shown.

Organizers

THE HOLD EVERYTHING BAG! (CONTINUED)
Wallet Zipper Pocket (CONTINUED)

Your zipper opening will look like this on the right side.

- On the back side of your pocket, place your zipper centered over the opening. You can either pin it in place or use basting tape.

FYI: While writing this book, I have fallen in love with basting tape, (Penny too!)

- On the right side with your zipper foot, stitch in the ditch all the way around your zipper box, starting and stopping on a long side.

- Fold your pocket in half and top stitch along the top folded edge to finish your zipper pocket.

Card & Top Pocket Assembly

- Make your pocket assembly. (see page 93.)

- Place pocket assembly 1 1/4" from the top edge of your wallet inside.

- Stitch along the bottom edge of the pocket assembly, sewing a scant 1/4".

- Fold your wallet inside fabric over the bottom edge of the pockets and sew a 1/4" tuck, encasing the bottom of the pocket assembly.

NOTE: *If your previous stitching shows, re-stitch your tuck with more seam allowance to hide previous stitching.*

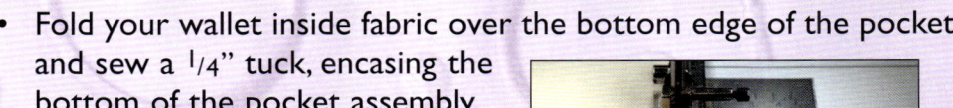

Organizers

THE HOLD EVERYTHING BAG! (CONTINUED)

Card & Top Pocket Assembly (CONTINUED)

- Once your wallet inside and wallet outside are completed with RST, sew along each side leaving the top and bottom open.

- Turn right side out, press flat and serge or zig-zag the top and bottom edges.

- Turn to page 12 for instructions on installing the wallet frame.

- After the wallet is completed, center it on the bag, 2" from the top edge of bag.

- To attach wallet to bag, sew along top edge just below the frame, using a narrow zipper foot.

- Sew along the edges on both sides and across the wallet, 1/4" above the center. This will allow ease when the frame is closed.

The Outside Double Pocket

This pocket is actually two pockets in one. They can hold your tablet, super-sized smart phone and/or anything else you might want to conceal and still have quick and easy access to. This pocket consists of a front side, which is padded and quilted and a back side, which is stiff.

Back Side of Pocket

- Make a sandwich of Deco-Magic® and your two pocket fabrics (11" x 10 1/2"). Fuse the Deco-Magic® to main fabric wrong side and fuse the lining fabric with Bonash Fusing Powder.

Organizers

THE HOLD EVERYTHING BAG! (CONTINUED)
Front Side of Pocket

- Fuse the pocket outside fabric (11" x 9") to Super Shaping Foam®, and quilt as you did for the bag outside.

- Use a pressing sheet to keep the back side from fusing to your ironing board. You can also use the single sided fusible here, but to keep things simple, I specified only one package of foam. Fuse to one side of foam only; use a pressing sheet on the other side of the foam to keep it from fusing to your pressing surface.

- Layer the quilted fabric with pocket lining, WST, but do not press.

- Sew one side of the zipper to the top edge of the pocket, with the teeth facing down. Serge raw edges, or use a zig-zag stitch along the zipper tape and top edge of bag.

- Fold pocket vent in half crosswise to measure 3 1/2" x 5 1/2".

- With the fold toward the top of the pocket, line vent up along the bottom and side edge with raw edges together and pin in place.

- Sew vent along the side edge with a 3/8" seam allowance.

- With right sides together, sew along the side with the vent, encasing the end of the zipper in the seam.

Organizers

THE HOLD EVERYTHING BAG! (CONTINUED)
Front Side of Pocket (CONTINUED)

- Your pocket will look like this from the right side, with the raw edge of the vent extending.

- Sew other side of the zipper tape to the top edge of pocket back, with right sides together.

- Marry zipper together.

- Top stitch along each edge of the zipper to keep seam allowances down. (Indicated by this dotted line.)

- Line up bottom edges and press the fold flat at the top so that the zipper teeth are about $1/2$" from the top.

- The back side of the pocket will extend $1/2$" on left.

- Pleat the vent inside the pocket, so that the raw edge is even with the back side of the pocket.

Organizers

THE HOLD EVERYTHING BAG! (CONTINUED)

Pocket Binding

- Sew binding along the two sides and bottom edges. (See Bias Binding in Basic Instructions, page 47.) Secure back side of binding with basting tape.

- Center pocket on bag with the top edge of the pocket 1/2" from the top edge of the bag.

- Stitch in the ditch, using an edge joining foot along both sides and along the bottom of the pocket.

HELPFUL HINT: *If you open the zipper, it is easier to sew along the vent side of the pocket.*

Sewing It All Together

- Sew the two sides starting where you stopped and sew bottom edge, but not the corners.

- Add bias binding to the bottom and finish the side bindings.

- To make the box corners of your bag, please refer to page 26.

Organizers

HOLD ANYTHING BASKET

Pam wanted a tote for all of her knitting supplies, so I created one with lots of outer pockets and then a large center opening. Once it was finished, everyone who saw it had a new use for it. One friend wants it for apple picking, another for sewing supplies and for me it will be perfect on my kitchen counter to 'catch' all those pens, notes and other odds and ends that never seem to have a home!

Supplies

- 1/2 yd Lining fabric
- 3/4 yd Outside fabric
- 1/3 yd back of pockets. (May use one of the above fabrics or a coordinating fabric.)
- 7 10" Squares of coordinating fabrics
- 2 1/4 yds Welt Cord
- 1 1/4 yd Micro Welt Cord
- 9" x 11" Deco-Magic®
- 12" x 48" Super Shaping Foam® Single Sided Fusible®
- 9" x 36" Heat n Stay Lite® Fusible Batting

Cutting

- Cut lining and outside fabrics per the diagrams to the right.

- From the remaining lining fabric, cut bias strips that are 2" wide. Cut at least 6 strips and use to create 2 strips measuring 2" x 40" each.

- Pocket pieces and bias for Micro Welt will be cut from the 10" squares during construction.

- Cut pocket backing fabric into 1 strip 5 1/2" x WOF and one piece 5 1/2" x 10". Stitch together on one 5 1/2" edge. Press. Set aside.

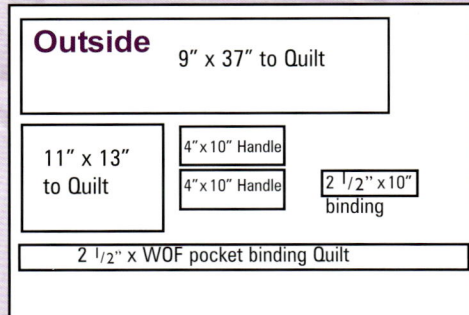

Lining
- 8" x 36" Lining Side
- 10" x 12" Lining Bottom — Use to cut bias fabric to cover welt cord

Outside
- 9" x 37" to Quilt
- 11" x 13" to Quilt
- 4" x 10" Handle
- 4" x 10" Handle
- 2 1/2" x 10" binding
- 2 1/2" x WOF pocket binding Quilt

Fabric provided by Moda Fabric Handmade by Bonnie and Camille

Organizers

HOLD ANYTHING BASKET

Construction - *All seams are 1/2" unless otherwise noted.*

- For the small pockets, take 2 of the 10" squares and cut each into 2 pieces measuring 4" x 5 1/2". I used 2 matching squares for this step. (4" wide x 5 1/2" high.)

- Take 4 more squares and cut each into a 9" x 5 1/2" piece. These are to be used for the larger outside pockets so you may want to do some 'fussy cutting'. (9" wide x 5 1/2" high.)

- For the 7th 10" square, follow the instructions on page 10 to create 1 1/2" bias strips. You will need to turn the entire 10" square into a 1 1/2" bias strip.

- Cover the 1 1/4 yd of Micro Welt Cord with this bias strip. Follow directions on page 55.

- Lay the wrong side of the pocket pieces on the fusible side of the Heat n Stay Lite® batting and fuse the batting to the fabric.

- Cut the pocket pieces apart.

- Stitch a piece of the covered Micro Welt Cord to the 5 1/2" side on the right of each pocket piece.

- Arrange the pocket pieces, alternating the large and small sizes.

- With WST, stitch the first pocket to the backing - leave at least 1" of backing on the left side of the pocket and stitch the pocket to the backing along the Micro Welt stitching line.

- Place the next pocket RST on top of this seam. Align edges and stitch again on the Micro Welt stitching line.

- Flip this pocket to the right and press in place.

- Continue stitching all of the pockets to the backing in the same manner.

- You should now have a strip of pockets with extra backing fabric on each side.

- On one side, trim the backing even with the edge of the pocket fabric.

Organizers

HOLD ANYTHING BASKET (CONTINUED)

Construction (CONTINUED)

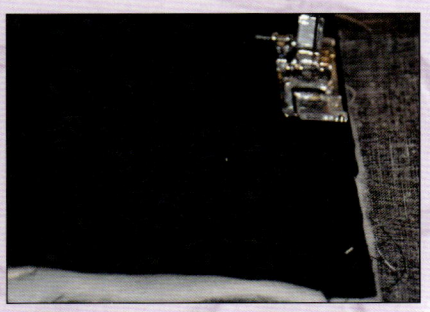

- Put the first and last pockets RST and stitch together.
- Trim the remaining backing fabric so that it extends 1" from the cut edge.
- You will use this extension to bind the edge of the seam.

- Press extension 1/2" toward the seam.
- Wrap this around the seam allowance and top stitch in place.
- Press bound seam to one side.

- Join the two pieces of binding fabric that you cut from the outside fabric.
- Press in half lengthwise and bind the top edge of the pocket band. I chose to stitch on the backing side and top stitch in place on the outside.
- Set pockets aside.

- Fuse the bottom and side pieces of the outside fabric to the Super Shaping Foam® and quilt. (See page 50.)
- Trim quilted pieces as follows: Bottom 10" x 12" and side 8" x 36".
- Use the 3" curve on the Seven Corner Ruler® to shape the four corners of the quilted bottom.
- Shape the lining bottom and the 9" x 11" piece of Deco-Magic® in the same manner.
- Fuse the Deco-Magic® to the wrong side of the lining bottom.

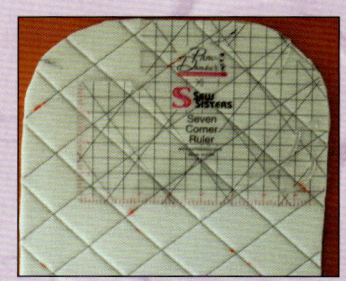

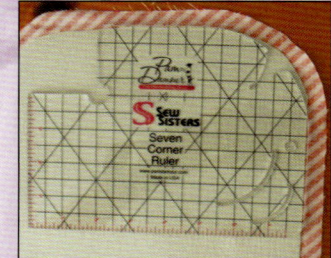

HOLD ANYTHING BASKET (CONTINUED)

Construction (CONTINUED)

- Stitch the side seam of the outside band and press open.

- Using the 2" bias that you created with the lining fabric, cover the 2 1/4 yds of Welt Cord. (See page 55.)

- Follow the instructions on page 55, stitch the covered Welt Cord to the top of the outside band.

- Divide the bottom of the outside band into quarters.

- Divide the bottom of the pocket section into quarters, using the centers of the large pockets for the marking points.

- Place the pocket section on top of the band and align the pins used to mark the quarter sections.

- Pin the small pockets in place onto the band.

- Tuck the large pockets on each side to fit in the remaining 6" spaces.

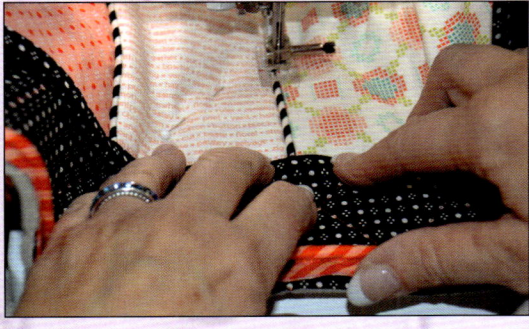

- Stitch pockets in place by stitching in the ditch along the edges of the Micro Welt stitching through all layers. Stitch along the bottom edge with a 1/4" seam.

- Stitch the remaining Welt Cord to the bottom edge of the band in the same manner as you did on the top of the band.

- Quarter the outside strip and the bag bottom. Align marking pins and pin or clip pieces together centering the large pockets at the center of each long side and each end.

- Clip curves on the band as needed to fit on the bottom.

- Using a welt cord foot stitch in place with the band on top.

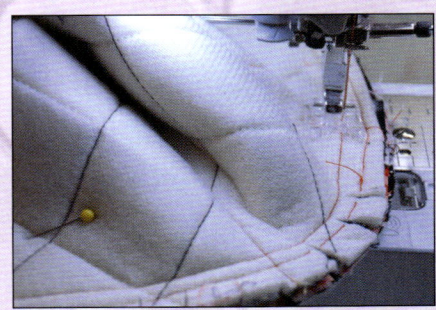

Organizers

HOLD ANYTHING BASKET (CONTINUED)
Construction (CONTINUED)

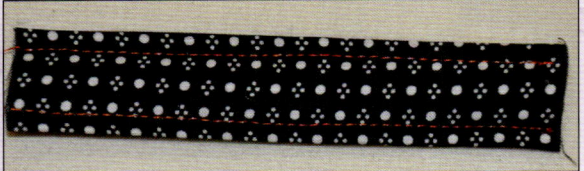

- Create bag handles following instructions for Double Folded Padded Straps page 46. For these handles, I used a 1" wide strip of Super Shaping Foam®.

- Topstitch handles with the same decorative thread used for quilting the band.

- Stitch handles to the ends of the bag, leaving 2" space between the inside edges of the handles.

- Stitch only the first and last inch of the side seam of lining band.

- Attach lining bottom to the lining band in the same manner that you did the outside bottom and band of the bag.

- With the bag inside out and the lining right side out, place the lining inside the bag and stitch along the top edge.

- Turn out through the hole you left in the side seam of the lining.

- Press lining to the inside along the top edge.

- Close the hole in the lining side seam by hand stitching or with Double Stick Tape®.

Organizers

MACRO WALLET

My wallet patterns have been such a success that we have developed an even larger frame to make those amazing long wallets, travel wallets and clutch purses. This pattern is fast, easy and gives you the perfect canvas for using leftover fabric, new techniques and/or new embellishments. Feel free to morph it to suit your own needs by adding more card pockets, outside pockets, or a strap.

Supplies

- Three coordinating fat quarters of quilting weight cottons
- One piece 10" x 9" Super Shaping Foam® Single Sided Fusible
- Two pieces of peel & stick pocket stabilizer: 10" x 3", 10" x 2 1/2"
- Bonash Bonding Powder and pressing sheet
- Lamé Stylo thread to match
- FriXion Pen
- 10" zipper tape with slide
- Hot glue gun and glue stick
- Flat Screwdriver
- Small 00 Phillips Head Screwdriver
- 10" Macro Wallet Frame

Cutting
As you cut, label each piece.

Main or outside fabric, cut rectangles:

- 11 1/2" x 9 1/2" Wallet outside
- 11" x 8" Zipper pocket
- 11" x 6 1/2" Top pocket

Fabric provided by Riley Blake Botanique Berry Collection

Wallet Inside	Zipper Pocket
Wallet Inside	Zipper Placket

Fabric #2

- 11" x 10" Wallet inside
- 11" x 8" Zipper pocket

Organizers

MACRO WALLET (CONTINUED)

Cutting (CONTINUED)

Fabric #3
- 11" x 2 1/2" Zipper placket
- 11" x 5 1/2" Card pocket

Pocket Stabilizer
Cut these Two Pieces
- 10" x 3"
- 10" x 2 1/2"

Construction

Outside

- Fuse the wrong side of wallet outside to the fusible side of Super Shaping Foam®, centering foam on the fabric with 3/4" extending on each end and about 1/4" top and bottom.

- Quilt with Lamé thread as desired. (You may choose to draw a grid with your FriXion Pen, free motion or outline quilt.) Set aside.

Pockets

- Fold top pocket and card pocket in half WST.

- Press and insert stabilizer centering on one half of pocket fabric, leaving 1/2" at each side and 1/4" at the bottom.

- Top stitch along the folded edges of each pocket section.

Organizers

MACRO WALLET (CONTINUED)

Pockets (CONTINUED)

- Line up the bottom edges of the two pocket sections and mark with your FriXion Pen for card pockets.

- Mark one line $1/2$" from each side edge, and 3 lines spaced $2\,1/2$" apart from the $1/2$" lines.

- Starting at the bottom of pockets, stitch up along one side of the three center lines, two stitches across the top and back down.

- Line up your pocket section so that it is $1\,1/4$" from the top edge of your pocket inside. Pin in place.

- Stitch $1/8$" along the bottom edge of pockets.

- Fold the wallet inside over the bottom edges of the pocket and sew to enclose the raw edges.

Zipper Pocket

- Fuse your two zipper pocket sections wrong sides together with Bonash Fusing Powder.

- Draw a zipper box on the wrong side of the zipper placket, drawing 1" all the way around from each edge. This will yield a box $1/2$" by 9". (See page 21.)

Organizers

MACRO WALLET (CONTINUED)
Zipper Pocket (CONTINUED)

- Line up the bottom edge of the placket 2" from the bottom edge of the zipper pocket.

- Sew along the zipper box, starting along one long side. **DO NOT SEW PAST THE CORNERS!** If you do sew past, rip it out! Otherwise your box will not lie flat.

- Draw a line down the center of your box, making a "Y" at each end.

- Cut along each side of the line, leaving a small gap opening as shown.

- Clip all the way to the corners without cutting the stitching.

- Pull placket fabric to the back, pleating at the ends. Press flat. (See photo on page 22.)

Organizers

MACRO WALLET (CONTINUED)

Zipper Pocket (CONTINUED)

- With the slide on your zipper, center the zipper onto the back of the opening.

- I use basting tape to help keep the zipper in place, or you can pin in place and stitch in the ditch all the way around.

- Trim the ends of the zipper so that they do not get sewn into the seam allowance.

- Fold pocket in half and top stitch folded edge.

Wallet Assembly

- Trim wallet outside to 11" by 9".

- Trim wallet inside to match.

- Here they are, lined up ready to sew together.

- Place zipper pocket section along the bottom edge and pin in place.

- With right sides together, sew along each side of the wallet, but NOT the top or bottom.

- Turn right side out and press flat.

- Serge or zig-zag top and bottom raw edges of wallet.

Installing the Frame

See page 12 for Wallet Frame installation.

79

Organizers

THE CELL PHONE WALLET

The Cell Phone Wallet has room for everything you need. Add a strap and it doubles as a small purse. The Mini Wallet is perfect for the person on the go. It's big enough to hold your ID, credit cards and cash, but it's small enough to fit in your pocket. Please read all the sewing directions and cutting instructions before beginning. Everything is written with $1/2$" seam allowances, unless otherwise specified. This wallet can accommodate the large iPhone 6s and the Galaxy note. It's also a perfect place for your passport! The cell phone pocket is 4 $1/4$" by 5 $1/2$".

Supplies

- $3/8$ yd of 3 coordinating fabrics or similar amounts of assorted scraps
- $1/4$ yd Super Shaping Foam® Single Sided Fusible
- 20" Zipper tape with 3 slides
- Peel and Stick or fusible stabilizer
- Small Wallet Clasp
- FriXion Pen or fabric marking pen/pencil
- Cell Phone/Mini Wallet Template
- Basting tape
- Size 00 Phillips Head Screwdriver
- Hot glue gun and glue stick
- 2 - $1/2$" D-rings and 60" purse chain
- Decorative thread for quilting
- Flat Head Screwdriver

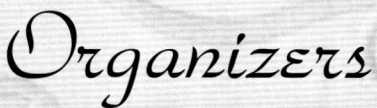

Organizers

THE CELL PHONE WALLET (CONTINUED)

Cutting Layout

Keep in mind, this layout is only a guideline for you. If you are using fat quarters or leftover fabric from your projects, you may be using anywhere from one to several fabrics. The beauty of my wallets is that they can be made from scraps!

Main Fabric (Floral/Outside)
- Wallet inside: 16" x 5 1/2"
- Card pocket: 16" x 5"
- Wallet body outside: 14" x 5 1/2" (Cut one)

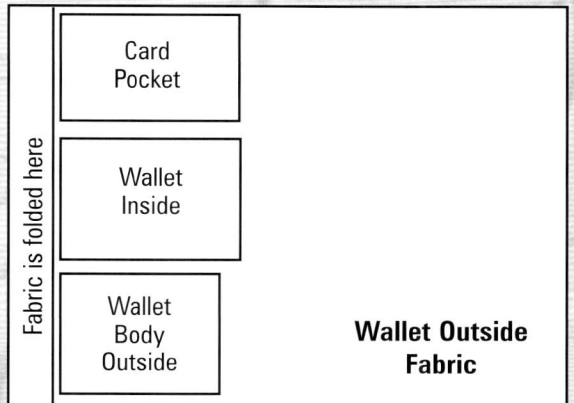

IMPORTANT TIP TO REMEMBER: *When using your template, remember to use the black placement lines for the Cell Phone Wallet and the pink lines for the Mini Wallet. All lines for the Cell Phone Wallet are cut on a fold, unless otherwise specified.*

Accent Fabric (Pink)
- Top pocket: 16" x 6 1/2"
- Wallet inside: 16" x 5 1/2"
- D-Ring loops: 2 1/2" x 8" (Cut 1 thickness, not on the fold)
- Cell phone pocket: 14" x 5 1/2"
- Optional outside zipper pocket: 10" x 5 1/2"

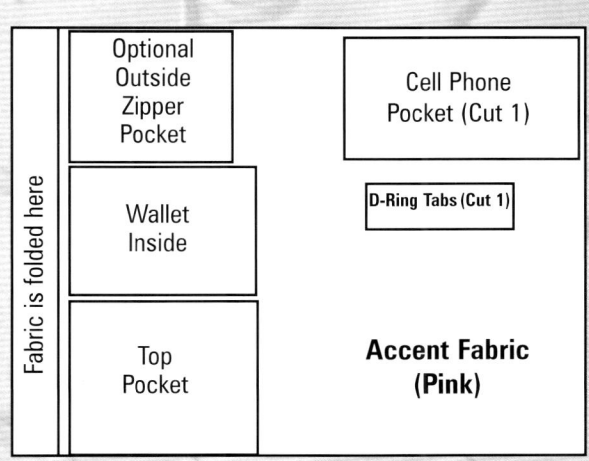

Organizers

THE CELL PHONE WALLET (CONTINUED)

Accent Fabric (Green)
- Zipper placket: 16" x 3"
- Card pocket: 16" x 5"
- Wallet inside: 16" x 5 1/2"

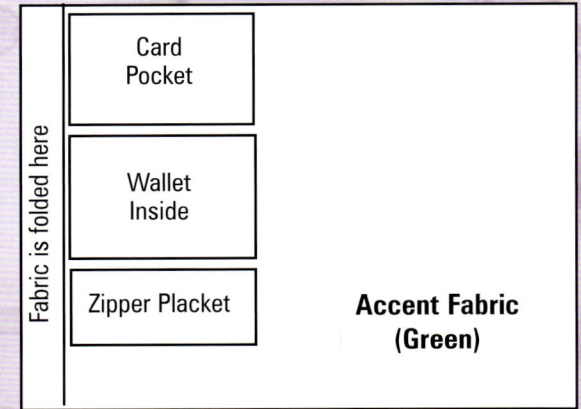

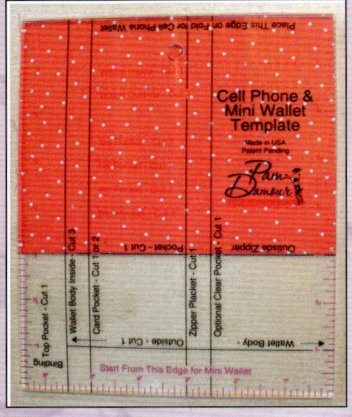 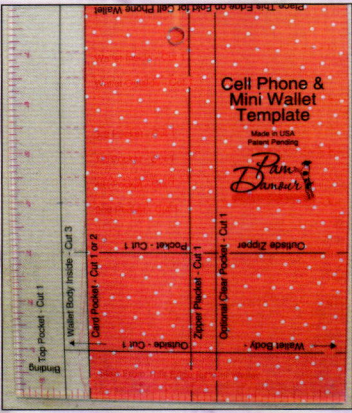

Here's how to use the Cellphone Template Ruler

NOTE: On my wallet template, after making a few of these, I have found it easier to place top edge of the template, (the end with the hang hole) at the cutting edge, and the black cutting lines on the fold of the fabric. All Mini Wallet cuts are cut single layer, not on the fold.

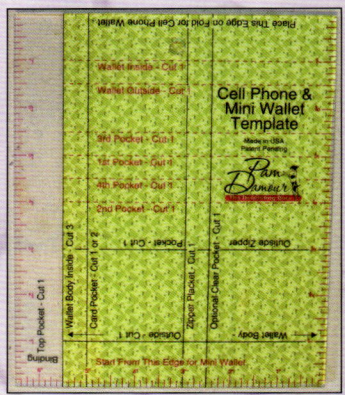 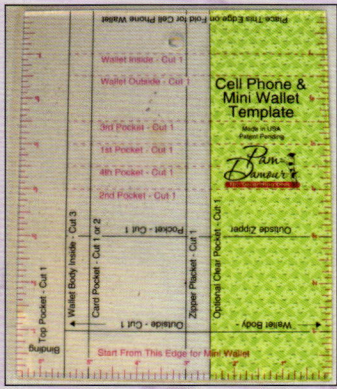

Super Shaping Foam®
- Cut 1 - 13 1/2" x 4 1/2"; 1 - 4 1/2" by 2 1/2"

Construction
- Fuse large Super Shaping Foam® to the wrong side of the wallet outside, lining up on one end. The foam will be 1/2" from the other three edges.

Organizers

THE CELL PHONE WALLET (CONTINUED)

Construction (CONTINUED)

- Fuse small Super Shaping Foam® to the wrong side of Cell Phone Pocket, at one end with ½" seam allowances on three sides.

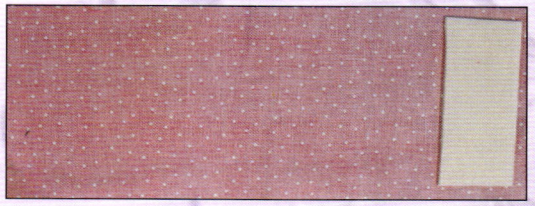

- With a FriXion Pen, mark quilting lines as desired. You can mark vertical, horizontal and or diagonally as shown by using the 60°/30° angle on a quilting ruler, use the Seven Corner Ruler® or you can use decorative stitches.

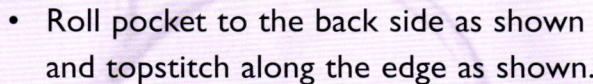

- Sew the un-quilted end of the pocket to the quilted end of the wallet body, using a ¼" seam allowance. It is folded under the wallet body here.

- Roll pocket to the back side as shown and topstitch along the edge as shown.

- Fold and pin so the pocket extends 2" past the outside wallet body. The entire piece should measure 16" long.

- Pin edges to secure and set aside.

THE CELL PHONE WALLET (CONTINUED)

Optional Outside Zipper Pocket

- To make the outside zipper pocket, draw a ½" zipper box, 1" from the top and side edges. Please refer to page 38 for complete instructions on how to make the Buttonhole Zipper Pocket.

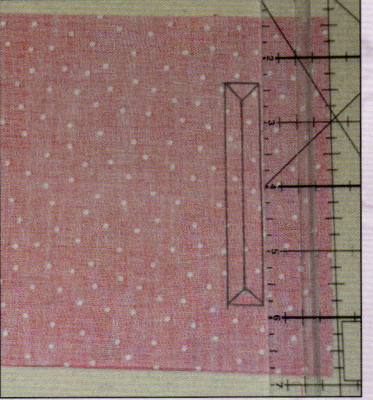

HELPFUL HINT: *If you have basting tape, place it on each side of the zipper to keep it in place as you sew.*

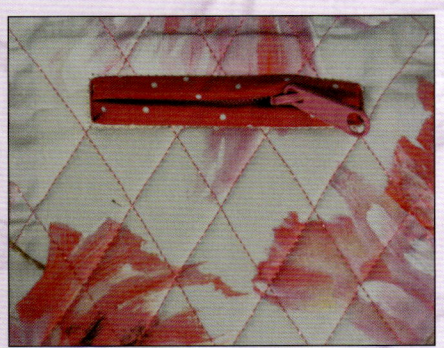

- Be sure to trim zipper ends so that they are at least ½" from the fabric edge.

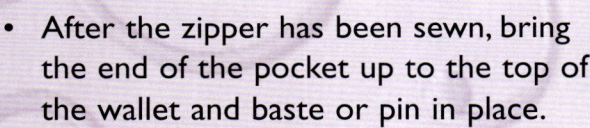

- After the zipper has been sewn, bring the end of the pocket up to the top of the wallet and baste or pin in place.

Inside Pockets

- Cut stabilizer to fit one half the depth of the pockets. Trim ½" off the ends and one side. (3 - 2" x 15")

- Stick or fuse in place.

- Fold in half lengthwise and press flat.

- Topstitch fold about ¼" from edge.

- Arrange pockets so that they are evenly spaced and sew at ¼" from the bottom edge. Sew each pocket section independently onto the top pocket section.

- Starting in the center out, mark for card pockets.

Organizers

THE CELL PHONE WALLET (CONTINUED)

Inside Pockets (CONTINUED)

- You can choose to make 4 card pockets on each side, or one section of mini card pockets which are also great for storing a USB stick, or a SD card.

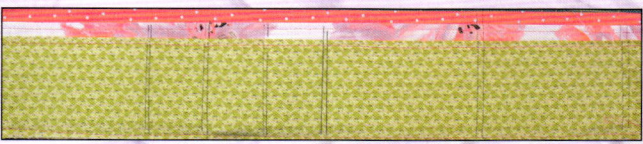

- Because of the size of wallet frame, mark off $1/2$" at each end, then divide each half in half, marking for 4 card pockets on each side. Or mark one side for mini card pockets. Each mini card pocket is $1\ 3/8$" wide, and each card pocket is $3\ 1/2$" wide. Do not make card pockets wider than $3\ 1/2$" as they will be too loose and card may slide out.

- Sew only the card pockets, but not the center divider. (You will sew down the center when the pockets are added to the wallet.) Starting at the bottom edge of wallet, sew up, make one stitch across the fold at the top of the pocket and stitch back down to the bottom. Set aside. (See diagram for stitching)

Buttonhole Zipper Pockets

- On the wrong side of the zipper placket fabric, draw a box down the center $1/2$" wide, stopping 1" from each side and each end. Turn to page 21 for zipper insertion.

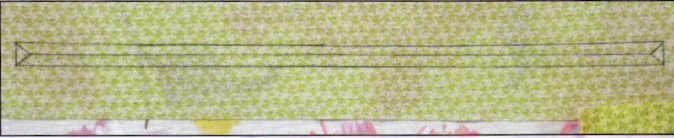

- This zipper will have two slides, creating two pockets. Cut 15" of zipper tape and insert 2 slides.

- With two slides on the zipper, sew zipper in place under placket.

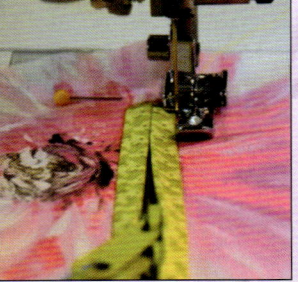

- After the zipper is sewn in place, trim loose ends of the zipper so it is at least $1/2$" from each end.

- Place last layer of wallet inside with right side up to the back of the zippered section. This will be the inside of the zipper pockets.

Organizers

THE CELL PHONE WALLET (CONTINUED)

Buttonhole Zipper Pockets (CONTINUED)

- Sandwich pocket section with lining and wallet outside. Pin in place.

- Stitch up and down the center of the pocket section, going through all layers and sewing all the way through the zipper placket.

Putting it all together!

- After your wallet outside is finished and your pocket assembly has been completed, sew together along the long sides only, leaving the ends open to turn.

HELPFUL HINT: Mark each of the long edges 1/2" from the edge. These lines should be 4 1/2" apart. Stitch on these lines.

- After turning, press flat using lots of steam. If you are not adding a strap, serge or zig-zag each end.

Optional D-rings and Strap

- Sew the D-ring strip into a tube with 1/2" seam allowances, or turn raw edges into the middle (like bias tape) and topstitch. Cut into two 3" sections. Fold in half over 1/2" D-rings.

- Place D-rings tabs 1/2" from each edge of the wallet. Stitch in place.

- Serge with a wide three thread overlock stitch or zig-zag all raw edges at each end of wallet.

Installing the Frame/Clasp

Please refer to page 12 for instructions on installing the Wallet Clasp.

- Fold your new wallet to close and press flat to set the memory in the fabric.

Variations

- Other variations include decorative stitching, serger stitching, embroidery. Add RFID fabric to protect your identity! Use leftover quilt blocks, scrap fabric, leather and more! Have fun with this! Make it your own!

Organizers

THE MINI WALLET

This wallet is tiny enough to fit in your back pocket, but has four pockets to hold cash, a credit card or two and your ID.

Supplies
- Two or three fat eighths of coordinating fabrics or similar amount of assorted scraps.
- Super Shaping Foam® 6 1/2" x 4 1/2"
- Peel & stick or fusible stabilizer
- Small Wallet Clasp
- FriXion Pen or fabric marking pen/pencil
- Cell Phone/Mini Wallet Template
- Size 00 Phillips Head Screwdriver
- Hot glue gun and glue stick
- Decorative thread for quilting
- Flat Head Screwdriver
- Basting Tape

Fabric Cutting
Cut one of each of the following
- 4 1/2" x 6 1/2" Wallet outside
- 4 1/2" x 7" Wallet inside
- 4 1/2" x 5" First pocket
- 4 1/2" x 4" Second pocket
- 4 1/2" x 5 1/2" Third pocket
- 4 1/2" x 4 1/2" Fourth pocket

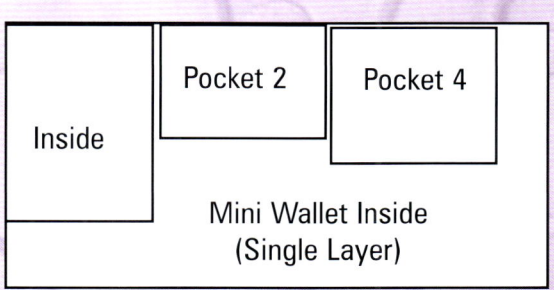

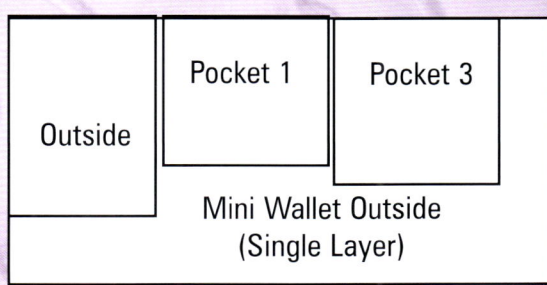

Stabilizer Cutting
Cut one each of the following
- 4 1/2" x 2"
- 1/2" x 2 1/4"
- 4 1/2" x 2 1/2"
- 4 1/2" x 2 3/4"

Construction
- Start by cutting pieces out using your wallet template. Each pocket is marked out with pink lines on your template. Cut one of each of wallet inside, outside, and pockets 1 to 4.

Organizers

THE MINI WALLET (CONTINUED)

Construction (CONTINUED)

- Using Super Shaping Foam®, cut one the size of the wallet outside. Trim off seam allowances on the width.
- Fuse to the wrong side of the wallet outside.
- Quilt as desired.
- Fold in half crosswise, and topstitch along the folded edge. Place stabilizer up to the fold and topstitch along the folded edge.

- Arrange the pockets on the wallet inside, with 1 & 2 on the top half of fabric, lining up at the bottom edges of pockets and about $3/4$" from the top edge.
- Sew along the bottom edges of the top pockets and bottom pockets about $1/4$".
- Fold the Wallet Inside crosswise at the bottom of the top pockets. Stitch along the fold with $1/4$" seam allowance. This will enclose the raw edges of the pocket bottoms. (See side view below.)

- With right sides together, sew along the sides with a $1/2$" seam allowance.
- Turn right sides out and press flat. Serge across top and bottom. Add hardware using instructions detailed on page 12.

Enjoy your new wallets!

P.S. I allow you to make these wallets for re-sale. Make them! Sell them! Enjoy them!

Organizers

THE POCKET WALLET

This wallet is just the right size to stick in your pocket, or small handbag, but big enough to carry all your essentials! It has 4 pockets for cards, a zippered pocket for change and an optional outer pocket for paper money and receipts. It can be easily cut using the pink lines on your wallet template. These lines were added for the cutting of the Pocket Wallet, which has a 4 1/2" clasp.

Supplies

- Three fat quarters of quilt fabric or coordinating scraps
- Super Shaping Foam® cut 4 1/2" x 8 1/2"
- Stabilizer for pockets
- Optional outside pocket - cut 8 1/2" x 10"
- Quick Clutch Wallet Template
- FriXion Pen
- Small Wallet Frame
- Size 00 Phillips Screwdriver
- Glue gun with glue
- Decorative thread
- 2 Zippers (13" of zipper tape and 2 slides)

Before you start

- You will still cut the same number of pockets (top pocket, card pockets, zipper pockets and zipper placket), but cut only to the pink line. The fabric will sit to the left of the pink line on the template.

- Use the pink zipper box for the inside zipper. If you wish to add an outside zipper pocket, use the black zipper box lines and cut one of the full size zipper plackets.

NOTE: You will need two zippers!

Or if you don't have the Quick Clutch Template, cut the following:

- Wallet outside - 5 1/2" x 8 1/2"
- Wallet inside - 5 1/2" x 9 1/2"
- Top pocket - 5 1/2" x 6 3/4"
- Zipper pocket - cut 4 - 5 1/2" x 4 3/8"
- Card pocket- cut 3 - 5 1/2" x 4"
- Inside zipper placket - 5 1/2" x 2 1/2"
- Optional outside zipper - 8 1/2" x 10"
- To make the optional outside zipper pocket, use the black zipper placket and zipper box lines. Cut one extra piece of wallet inside fabric to line the large outside pocket.

Fabric provided by Maywood Studios, Catalina Ultra Violet Collection

Organizers

THE POCKET WALLET (CONTINUED)

Construction

Wallet Outside

- Center Super Shaping Foam® on the wrong side of wallet outside, and fuse in place.

- Quilt as desired.

- If making the optional zipper pocket, draw a zipper box on pocket fabric, making the top edge of the box 1 1/2" from the side edge of wallet.

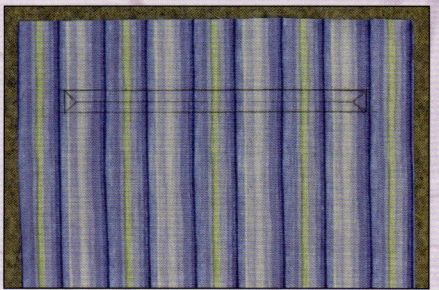

- Place along one of the long sides of wallet outside, RST together and make Buttonhole Zipper Pocket. (See page 38.)

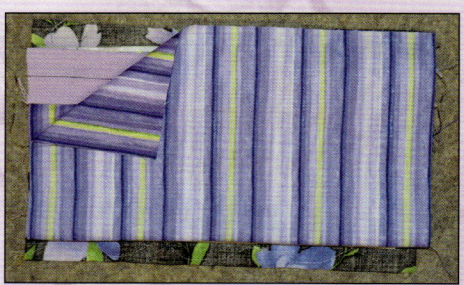

- After inserting zipper, fold opposite end over, RST with the edge lined up with the edge of wallet outside.

- Set aside.

Wallet Inside

- Construct the inside just as you would following the instructions for the Quick Clutch Wallet. (Starting on page 92.)

- Begin with the top and card pockets, adding stabilizer. Topstitch along the folded edges.

- Place pocket assembly 3/4" from the top edge of wallet inside fabric. Stitch along the bottom edge of pocket assembly.

- Fold bottom of wallet inside over and stitch a tuck to enclose the raw edges of your pocket assembly.

- Press flat.

Organizers

THE POCKET WALLET (CONTINUED)

Construction

Wallet Inside (CONTINUED)

- Make the zipper pocket using instructions for the Quick Clutch Wallet. (See page 95.)

- With RST, sew wallet outside to wallet inside, along foam edges. Do not sew foam into the seam.

NOTE: *if you want to protect your identity with RFID Fabric, add a layer before you sew the outside edges. Layer it against the wrong side of the wallet inside assembly portion of your wallet.*

- Turn right side out, press flat and serge edges.

- Install frame. (See page 12.)

91

Organizers

THE QUICK CLUTCH WALLET

This wallet is fun and easy to make. Using our wallet template, there is no measuring and cutting is quick and easy. Its quilted cover gives it a rich sturdy feel, and it has two large pockets for bills and/or checkbooks. There are 6 card pockets and a zippered pocket for coins. The finished size when folded is 7 1/2" by 4 1/4". The metal fame is easy to install with 8 tiny screws to hold everything in place.

Supplies

- Three fat quarters of coordinating fabrics or similar amounts of assorted scraps. (I used 5 scraps to make this sample.)
- 7 1/2" x 8 1/2" Super Shaping Foam® Single Sided Fusible
- 8" Zipper tape with 1 slide
- Peel & stick or fusible stabilizer
- 7 1/2" Clutch Frame
- FriXion pen or fabric marking pen/pencil
- Quick Clutch Wallet Template
- Size 00 Phillips Head Screwdriver
- Hot glue gun and glue
- Small Flat Head Screwdriver

Cutting
When cutting, use the appropriate line for each section on the template

- Body outside: 1 - 9" by 9"
- Super Shaping Foam® : 1 - 7 1/2" by 8 1/2"
- Wallet lining: 1 - 8 1/2" by 9 1/2"
- Zipper pocket: 4 - using the Quick Clutch Ruler or cut 8 1/2" x 4 1/2" in fabrics of your choice
- Top pocket: 1 - using the Quick Clutch Ruler or cut 8 1/2" x 6 3/4"
- Card pockets: one of each fabric - using the Quick Clutch Ruler or cut 8 1/2" x 4"
- Zipper placket: cut one - using the Quick Clutch Ruler of 8 1/2" x 2 1/2"
- Pen loop: cut one - using the Quick Clutch Ruler or cut 2" by 2 1/2"
- Stabilizer: 3 - 2" x 7 1/2" for card pockets; 3 3/4" x 7 1/2" for zipper pocket; and 3" x 7 1/2" for the top pocket.
- Label all pieces after cutting.

Organizers

THE QUICK CLUTCH WALLET (CONTINUED)

Construction

- Begin by fusing the 9" fabric square to the Super Shaping Foam®, wrong sides together. (The rough side of the shaping foam is the fusible side.)

- Next, draw a 1 1/4" grid with fabric marking pen, chalk or FriXion Pen on the right side of outer body fabric, or using the first line for the Center Strip, mark grid lines. Stitch on the gridlines.

- Use Wallet Template to trim to size. Set aside.

Pockets

- Begin with the top pocket. This is how you use the wallet template. To cut the pockets, align the cut edge of the fabric with the corresponding lines on the template. Each template line will indicate the number of pieces to cut.

- Apply stabilizer to the back side, and fold in half with wrong sides together. The stabilizer will be about 1/2" from the cut edge of the pocket.

- Top stitch 1/4" from folded edge.

- Apply stabilizer to remaining three card pocket rectangles. Fold in half with wrong sides together to make three 8 1/2" wide pockets. You can make one pocket of each of your three fat quarters or use scraps as shown here, with 5 coordinating fabrics.

- Top stitch 1/4" from folded edge on each pocket.

- Begin with one of the card pockets and position 3/8" from the top edge of the Top pocket.

- Stitch along the bottom edge of the card pocket, about 1/4" from the bottom edge of card pocket.

- Repeat with second and third card pockets.

NOTE: You may need to adjust pockets slightly to keep them evenly spaced.

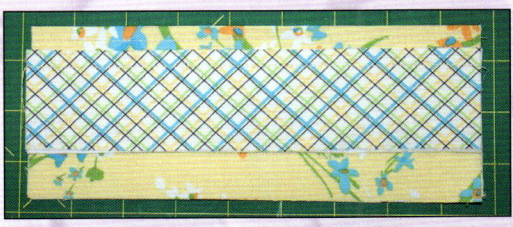

Organizers

THE QUICK CLUTCH WALLET (CONTINUED)

- The bottom card pocket should line up evenly with the bottom of the large Top Pocket.

- Using the Wallet Template, draw a line in the center to mark your stitching line for the card pockets.

- Sew up the center along each side of center mark to make six card pockets, as shown here by the dotted line.

Wallet Lining

- Pin pocket section to the top edge of wallet lining, with the top edge of the pockets 1" from the top edge.

- The bottom of the pockets should be just above the center line. Stitch in place at 1/4" from edge.

Pen Loop

- Cut pen loop from the template.

- Fold each edge under along the shorter side, then fold in half. Stitch along folded edges to make pen loop.

- Fold loop in half, and place raw edges of pen loop centered on the bottom edge of the pocket assembly.

- Fold wallet lining over the bottom of the card assembly and pin or hold in place with Wonder Clips.

- Stitch along the previous stitching line, creating a tuck to encase all the raw edges.

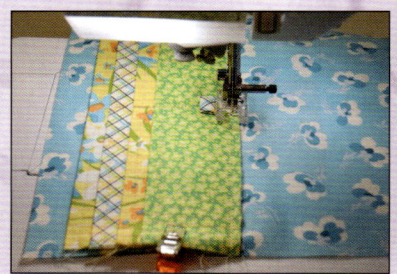
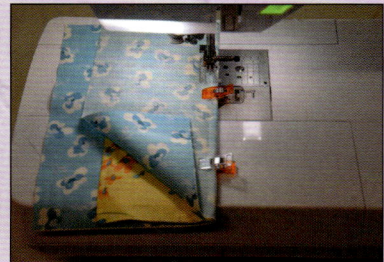

Organizers

THE QUICK CLUTCH WALLET (CONTINUED)

Zipper Pocket

- This wallet has the Buttonhole Zipper Placket insertion. Please refer to page 21 for complete instructions.

- With the last two zipper pocket pieces, make a sandwich by placing wrong sides together, to make the zipper pocket back.

- Sew zipper pocket back to the zipper pocket front at the top edge, using a $1/2$" seam allowance.

- Press seam open. Optional: Topstitch down $1/4$" from the top edge.

- Pin or Wonder Clip the zipper pocket to the bottom half of the wallet lining.

Assembly

Now you are ready to put your wallet together. Put right sides together and pin to prevent slipping.

- Sew along sides only with a SCANT $1/2$" seam allowance.

- The overall finished width should be $7 1/2$".

- Measure before stitching to make sure your wallet will fit your frame.

- Turn right sides out and press flat.

Finishing

- Once your wallet is turned right sides out and pressed, it is time to put your frame or clasp on.

- Please refer to page 12 for complete instructions on how to install the hardware.

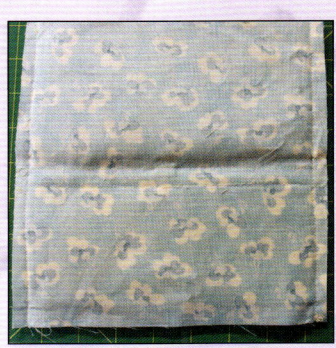

Organizers

THE QUICK CLUTCH WALLET VARIATIONS

Evening Clutch

- Other variations include: decorative stitching, serger stitching, embroidery and Zentangle inspired fabric.

- To make an evening bag like this one, cut your project 12" long instead of the length of the template. The inside pockets can be made deeper to accommodate cell phone, makeup and other necessities. An optional wristlet strap or shoulder strap can be added by sewing into the side seams before the final assembly. This bag has a velvet exterior, with Austrian crystals in the quilting intersections.

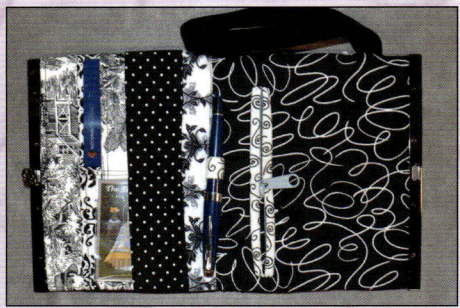 

- Another variation is this art supply wallet. I added Zentangle to the outside of this project and an outside zipper to hold more pens.

Art Supply Wallet

  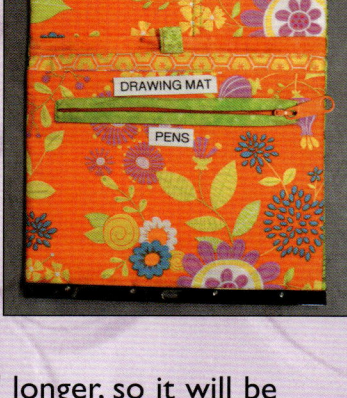

- Another variation is to add an outside pocket for your cell phone and/or a chain. To accommodate a larger cell phone, make 1" to 2" longer, so it will be a deeper wallet.

Organizers

THE ELEGANT ORGANIZER

This sweet little bag can be dressed up or down depending on the fabrics you use. Here, we chose to use Cuddle Suede by Shannon Fabrics to give it a luxurious feel. The optional embroidery adds a bit of whimsy.

Supplies
- 1/3 yd Cuddle Suede (or outside fabric of your choice)
- 1/2 yd Lining fabric
- 1/4 Accent fabric #1
- 1/4 Accent fabric #2
- 3/8 yd Nylon organza for embroidered flower
- Optional: 6" square of Texture Magic™ or Heat N Shrink® for flower center
- Matching thread
- 10" Wallet clasp
- 60" Purse chain with 2 D-rings
- 20" of Zipper tape with 2 slides
- Deco-Magic®: 2 - 10" x 5 3/4", 2 - 2 1/2" x 10"
- Plastic canvas: 1 - 2 1/2" x 10"
- 4 Bag feet
- Basting tape
- Décor-Bond® or Perfect Stick®
- Wonder Clips
- 21 1/2" x 10" Stabilizer for pocket

Cuddle Suede fabric provided by Shannon Fabrics

Cutting
Cuddle Suede Fabric
- Bag outside: 1 - 11" x 14"
- Sides: 2 using the print-out pattern on the CD

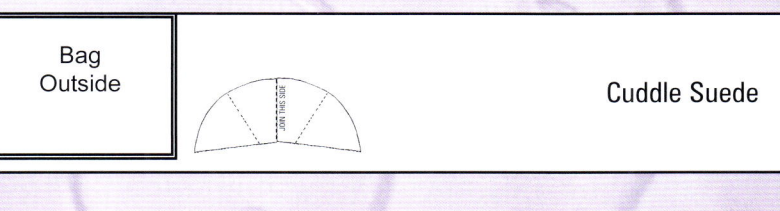

Lining & Inside Pockets
- Bag inside lining: 1 - 11" x 16"
- Card pocket: 1 - 11" x 4"
- Dividing zipper pocket: 2 - 10" x 8"
- Sides: 2 using the print-out pattern on the CD
- D-ring tabs: 2 - 2" x 4"
- Zipper pocket: 5" x 11"

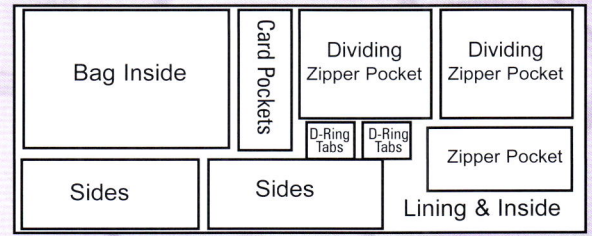

Accent #1: (Polka Dot)
- Top pocket: 7" x 11"
- Card pocket: 11" x 4"
- Zipper placket: 2 1/2" x 11"
- Zipper pocket: 5" x 11"

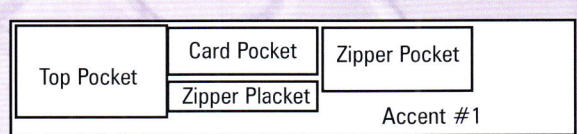

Organizers

THE ELEGANT ORGANIZER (CONTINUED)

Accent #2 - (Large Floral)
- Card pocket: 11" x 4"
- Zipper Pocket: 2 - 5" x 11"

Zipper Pocket	Zipper Pocket	Card Pocket
		Accent #2

Deco-Magic®
- Bag front & back: 2 - 10" x 5 ¾"
- Bag bottom: 2 - 2 ½" x 10"

Plastic Canvas
- 2 ½" x 10" for bag bottom

Stabilizer (Such as a peel & stick, or Décor Bond)
- 3 - 2" x 10"
- 1 - 3 ½" x 10" for top pockets
- 1 - 4" x 10" for zipper pocket
- 1 - 8" x 10" for dividing zipper pocket
- 2 – Using the print-out pattern

Construction

Bag Outside

- Fuse three pieces of the Deco-Magic® to the outside bag fabric. (Cuddle Suede.) The larger pieces will line up evenly at the ends, with ½" of fabric extending on each side.

- Fuse the other layer of the Deco-Magic® to the plastic canvas.

- Place the plastic canvas and Deco-Magic® on the bag bottom section to help reinforce and retain the shape of the bag.

- Mark for feet 1" from the side edge of the Deco-Magic®, ½" from the front & back edges. See page 14 for more detailed instructions on Bag Feet.

- Make a hole with your seam ripper for the feet prongs to pass through.

- Slide the backing disk over the prongs and spread prongs open to secure feet.

- Set aside.

Organizers

THE ELEGANT ORGANIZER (CONTINUED)

Construction (CONTINUED)
Card Pockets

- This organizer has card pockets which consist of three levels of card pockets sewn onto a larger top pocket.

- Fold all three card pockets and the top pocket in half lengthwise. Insert stabilizer on one half of each pocket. Center stabilizer so that it starts 1/2" from each edge.

- Top stitch 1/4" from the edge along the folded edges of all four pieces.

- Sew each section onto the top pocket at the bottom edge with a 1/4" SA, spacing evenly with the folded edges all about 3/8" apart.

- Mark for your card pockets. At each edge, mark a line 1/2" from the edge. (This is the seam allowance at the sides of your bag.)

- Make the next line 1 1/4" over from the 1/2" mark. Make the next line 1 1/4", the next 3 3/4" and you should have another 3 3/4" to the last marked line.

- Sew the fourth line only starting at the bottom of the pockets, sew up to the top of the third folded edge, pivot and sew back down to the bottom.

- Mark the center of the wallet inside, and 1 1/4" on each side, so you have your 2 1/2" bottom area marked out.

- Place pocket assembly onto the wallet inside, 2" from the top edge. Pin in place and stitch along the bottom edge of the pockets.

- Sew up lines 2 and 3 to make mini pockets for USB stick, SD cards and all those keychain cards.

- Fold the wallet inside over the pocket assembly bottom, and stitch a tuck to enclose all the pocket raw edges. Set aside.

Zipper Pocket

- This pocket uses our signature "Buttonhole Zipper" insertion. (Please refer to page 21 for complete instructions.)

- On the zipper placket wrong side, mark a zipper box, 1/2" wide by 9" long. There should be 1" of fabric all the way around the box.

Organizers

THE ELEGANT ORGANIZER (CONTINUED)

Construction

Zipper Pocket (CONTINUED)

- Stabilize one of the zipper pocket fabrics with either Décor-Bond® or Perfect Stick®, leaving $1/2$" seam allowances all the way around.

- With WST, sandwich the stabilized zipper pocket piece to one of your other zipper pocket pieces.

- With RST, lining up the top edges, place the zipper placket on the stabilized zipper pocket piece. Please refer to page 21 complete instructions.

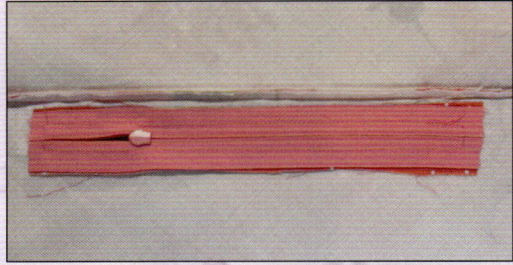

- With WST, make a "pocket sandwich" with the two remaining zipper pocket pieces.

- Pin "pocket sandwich" to the pocket piece with the buttonhole zipper opening, with RST.

- Sew along the top edge. Press seam and fold in half with seam at the top edge.

- Place the zipper pocket along the opposite edge of your bag inside, $1\ 1/4$" from the end. Because this is a purse, and not a wallet, you will want the pockets to open in opposite directions.

- Sew with a $1/4$" seam allowance along the bottom of the zipper pocket.

- Stitch a tuck to enclose all the pocket raw edges, like you did for the card pockets.

- Measure your wallet inside. If it still measures more than 14", trim excess off on the card pocket end.

Organizers

THE ELEGANT ORGANIZER (CONTINUED)

Construction
Bag Sides

- Print out pattern from CD for this section. Cut out stabilizer using the stabilizer pattern, which is 1/2" smaller all the way around.

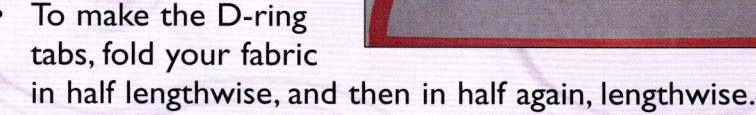

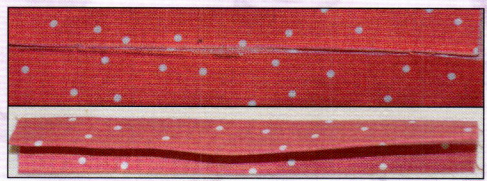

- To make the D-ring tabs, fold your fabric in half lengthwise, and then in half again, lengthwise.

- Stitch closed along the folded edges.

- Slide the D-ring onto each tab, and pin into place on the center, with raw edges together.

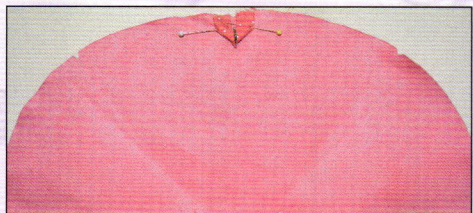

- With RST, pin the lining of the bag side to the outer fabric. Sew along the curve edge.

- Trim 2/3 of the seam allowance off, turn right sides out and press flat.

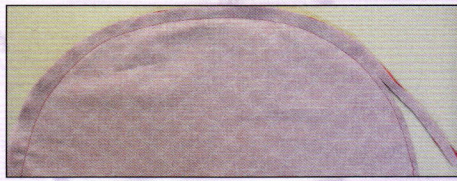

- Pin the bag sides to the bag inside on each side. Baste in place.

- With RST, pin bag outside to the bag inside, sewing only on the sides.

- Turn RSO and press.

- Using the dotted lines on your pattern, mark for accordion darts.

Organizers

THE ELEGANT ORGANIZER (CONTINUED)

Construction

Zippered Dividing Pocket

Follow the instructions on page 40 for the zippered dividing pocket.

Finishing

- With Wonder Clips holding the edges folded, and the bag turned inside out, sew a dart, starting at $1/2$" at the top and taper to nothing as you approach the bottom of the bag.

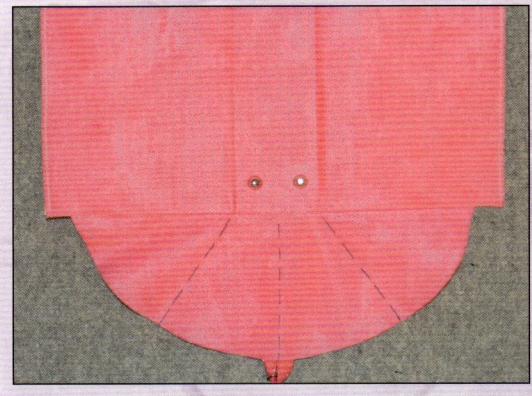

- Repeat on the opposite side.

- Prepare the dividing pocket, as shown on Page 40.

- You will be sewing your zipper along the 10" sides.

- Serge ends of dividing pocket.

- With Wonder clips, pinch the side, with the dividing pocket caught in the fold. Sew another dart, starting at $1/2$" at the top, and tapering as you approach the bag bottom.

- Serge the two top edges of your bag, and install frame, using directions shown on page 12.

Organizers

THE ZIPPER POCKET BAG

This sweet little bag is a great way to use up extra zippers. It has three different compartments. The ric-rac strap looks like a twisted rope. It can be made from one or more fabrics, or fabric and zipper scraps.

Fabric & Supplies

Fabric: 3/8 yard of one fabric, or assorted scraps
- Bag back: Cut 2 - 11" x 9"
- Cut 1st pocket - 12 1/2" x 11"
- Cut 2nd pocket - 10 1/2" x 11"
- Cut 2 Strap tabs - 2" x 4"
- Super Shaping Foam® - 10" x 8"
- 8 Assorted zippers cut 11" with 3 slides
- 2 Snap hooks & D-rings with 3/4" inside opening
- 2 - 45" pieces of large ric-rac
- Matching thread
- 1/4" Basting tape

Fabric provided by Riley Blake, Botanique Berry Collection

Construction

Bag Back

- With wrong sides together, press your fabric back pieces with Super Shaping Foam® in the center, sew with 1/2" of seam allowance all the way around.

- Quilt using your desired pattern. Set aside.

Bag Front

- Cut zipper pieces to size and arrange in desired order.

- Place basting tape on the top edge of the 7 lower zipper pieces. (The first zipper at the top will not need the tape.)

- Fold your first pocket in half. Place the folded edge even with the top edge of your third zipper.

- Using basting tape, place the first zipper over the edge of the second, so that the teeth are 3/4" apart. Place the second zipper over the edge of the third.

Organizers

THE ZIPPER POCKET BAG (CONTINUED)

Bag Front (CONTINUED)

- Sew between the zipper teeth, stitching zippers 1 & 2, and 2 & 3 with a zig-zag or decorative stitch. I chose to use a pink variegated thread for a more decorative effect.

- Line up 2nd pocket folded edge to the top edge of the fourth zipper.

- Separate the third zipper (the pink one on our sample) and stick onto the top edge of fourth zipper using basting tape.

- Sew as before, between the teeth of the third and fourth zippers.

- Separate the fourth zipper, and sew the bottom section onto the top of the fifth zipper.

- Continue to sew the sixth, seventh and eighth zippers in the same manner, spacing each with teeth 3/4" apart.

- With one of the zipper slides, marry the third and fourth zippers back together.

- Sew the bag back to the top edge of the first zipper, with right sides together, with a 1/2" seam allowance. Serge or zig-zag the seam edges.

- Insert slides onto the first, third and fourth zippers. You may choose to insert them all on the same side or opposite sides as shown here.

- The bag should measure about 16", with the back of the bag 1" larger than the front (zipper) side.

- Line up the bottom edges only, and sew with a 1/2" seam allowance. Serge or zig-zag the bottom edge.

Organizers

THE ZIPPER POCKET BAG (CONTINUED)

Strap Tabs

- Make strap tabs as shown. Bring folded edges together and top stitch both sides.

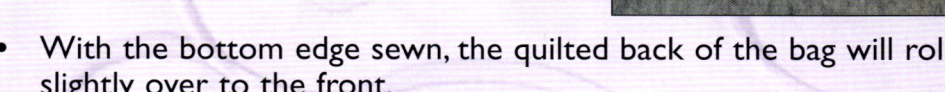

- Slide tab through D-ring and fold in half with ends together.

- With the bottom edge sewn, the quilted back of the bag will roll slightly over to the front.

- Finger press flat, and insert each strap tab into the sides at the top edge.

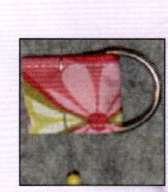 

- Pin tab with D-ring in place and sew sides, attaching the strap tab at the same time. Reinforce stitching at the tabs.

- Serge or zig-zag to finish edges.

- Turn right side out and press flat.

Strap

- To make strap, wrap two pieces of large ric-rac together as shown. Press flat and sew down the center. Sew one more row of stitching $1/4$" on each side of center.

- Wrap raw ends of strap under, folding over the opening of the snap hook, and stitch along the fold.

- Snap strap onto your bag and you are done!

With a Little Help from our Friends

DE-DE'S BAG

This bag was created by Diane H. Murphy at one of our boot camp retreats. It's the perfect size for everyday use, not too large, not too small. I loved it so much, I asked her to make one for me!

It uses quilting weight fabrics, quilted with our own fusible bag batting interfacing. There are a couple of variations for closures and pockets, so you can really make it own.

Supplies

- 3/4 yard main bag body outside
- 1/2 yard bag inside lining
- 3/8 yard each of three coordinating solid fabrics
- Super Shaping Foam® double side fusible (small size: 18" x 58")
- 1 Swivel clip
- FriXion Pen
- Decorative thread (optional)
- 2 pieces 4 1/4" x 10 3/4" of Deco-Magic® for bag bottom
- 26" of zipper tape and three slides
- 4 Bag feet
- Seven Corner Ruler®
- Clover Pressing Finger
- # 6 Fasturn Tube Turner

Cutting

Main Bag Outside Fabric (Shown here folded in half lengthwise, for double thickness.)

- Bag body 2 - 10" x 16"
- Straps 2 - 24" x 3 1/2"
- Two-Way Top Zipper Placket: 2 - 4 1/2" x 12"
- Loop for Key Fob: 1 - 6" x 2"
- Hanging Quilted Pocket binding: 2 - 3" x 7 1/2"
- Quilted Double Pocket binding: 1 cut on bias: 23" x 2"
- Bag bottom: 1 - 12" x 5 1/4" (FYI: We used solid black, but this can also be cut from the outside fabric.)
- Zipper tab: 2 - 2" x 2"

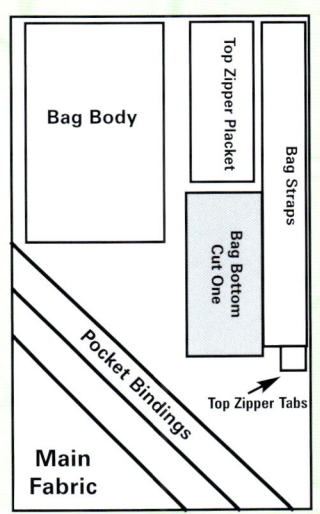

Yellow Lining Fabric (single thickness)

- Bag body lining 2 - 10" x 16"
- Bag bottom 12" x 5 1/4"
- Decorative banding: cut two at 2" x 17"
- Inside binding: cut two 9 1/2" x 2"
- Inside bottom edge binding: 1 - 32" x 2 1/2"

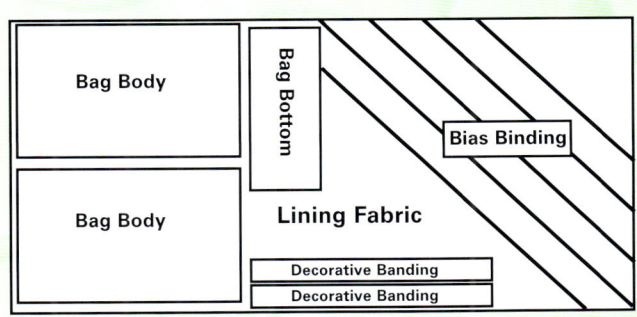

107

DE-DE'S BAG (CONTINUED)

Green Accent Fabric
- Cut one piece 14" x 9" for Hanging
- Decorative banding: 2 - 2" x 17"
- Hanging Quilted Pocket: 1 - 16" x 8 ½"

Purple Accent Fabric
- Hanging Zipper Pocket: 1 - 15 ½" x 9"
- Decorative banding: 2 - 2" x 17"
- Hanging Quilted Pocket binding: 1 - 2 ½" x 8 ½"

Teal Accent Fabric
- Hanging Quilted Pocket: 1 - 11" x 8 ½"
- Decorative banding: 2 - 2" x 17"
- Top binding: 1 - 3" by 32"

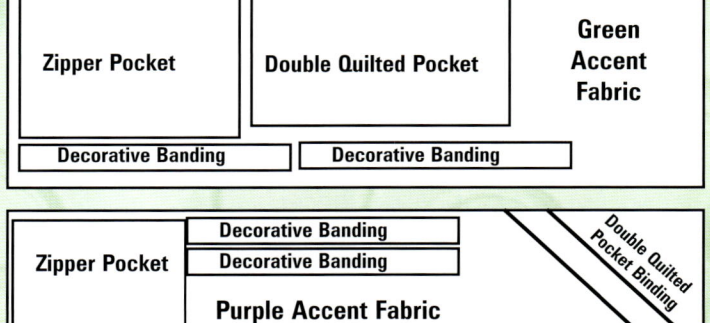

Bag Bottom
(Black Solid if not using main fabric)
- 1 - 12" x 5 ¼"

Deco-Magic®
- 1 - 11" by 4 ¼"

Super Shaping Foam®
- 2 - 10" x 16" for bag body
- 2 - 1 ¼" x 24" for straps
- 1 - 7 ¾" x 8 ½" and 1 - 5 ¼" x 8 ½" for Hanging Quilted Pocket

Construction

- Begin by completing each section of the bag, then you will put it all together.

- Sandwich your bag outside fabric and inside fabric with your Super Shaping Foam® and press to fuse the three layers together.

- Mark for quilting lines with the Frixion Pen, using the quilting guide on the Seven Corner Ruler® or use one of the 45° or 60° lines on one of your quilting rulers. Quilt with your choice of decorative threads and set aside. (For directions on marking and quilting, please turn to page 50 of basic instructions.)

With a Little Help from our Friends

DE-DE'S BAG (CONTINUED)

Construction (CONTINUED)

- Make the Hanging Zipper Pocket and Hanging Quilted Pocket, following directions on pages 29 & 31.

Bag Embellishment

- This bag can be embellished with bias trim, embroidery or other variations.

Here are a few ideas:

- By making your own bias trim, you can create fun effects such as the two shown here. Use these designs or create your own for your bag. Top stitch in place.

Key Fob

- Do you like the idea of having a key fob in your bag? Turn to page 15 to see how to make this!

Two Way Top Zipper Placket

- Please refer to page 23 for directions on making the Two Way Top Zipper Placket.

109

DE-DE'S BAG (CONTINUED)

Bag Bottom

- Fuse the Deco-Magic® to the wrong side of bag bottom, centering, leaving $1/2$" seam allowance all the way around.

- Measure 1" from each corner of the Deco-Magic®, and mark for your bag feet. (See page 14.)

- Use the back plate as a guide to cut two slots in each corner for the bag feet prongs.

- From the right side, put prongs through slits to the back, while going through the back of the plate.

- Open prongs and spread flat to secure.

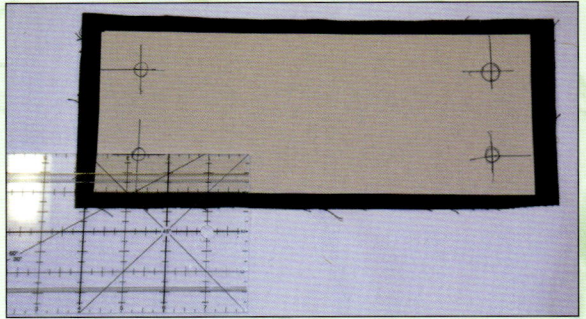

Padded Strap

See page 45 for instructions.

Top Binding

- Cut your binding and press raw edges inside to make a double fold bias tape. (See page 47.)

Bag Assembly

- Lay out your pieces as shown here.
- Pin or baste each pocket to each side of the bag at the top edge.
- Sew bag sides only, using the bias binding method.
- Pin straps with outside edge of strap 3" from each side seam.

DE-DE'S BAG (CONTINUED)

Bag Assembly (CONTINUED)

- Finish seams using the bias binding method. (See page 47.) You will not have to finish the ends because they will be encased in the top and bottom finishes.

- Using pins, mark the center of each side of the bag and of each side of bag bottom.

- Pin bag at center sides and ends.

- Sew with a 1/2" seam allowance, adding the binding as you sew, with all the raw edges together.

- Fold over raw edges at ends.

- Wrap folded edge of binding over and top stitch in place.

- With the two zipper placket sections pinned to each side of the bag top, baste top edges to secure zipper plackets, pockets and key fob.

- Sew binding to the top edge just as you did on the bottom from the inside of the bag. Wrap to the outside of the bag and top stitch in place.

With a Little Help from our Friends

JACLYN'S BAG

This is a bag of many possibilities! It's a lunch bag. It's a cosmetic bag. Add a strap and it's a great little purse! It's whatever you want it to be!

Supplies

- 1/2 yd Outside fabric
- 3/8 yd Lining
- 1/4 yd Accent fabric
- 15" x 17" Deco-Magic Lite®
- 17" Zipper tape with 2 slides
- Construction thread and decorative accent thread
- 1 1/4 yd Micro Welt Cord
- Wonder Clips
- Optional 60" bag chain

Fabric provided by Maywood Studios Catalina Ultra Violet Collection

Cutting Instructions

- Cut and label all pieces.

Outside Fabric

- 8 1/2" x 10 1/2" Bag front and bag back
- 2 Sides – Pattern on the CD
- 8 1/2" x 6" Outer back pocket
- 8 1/2" x 6" Inside pocket lining
- 2" x 8" for Strap tabs

Lining Fabric

- 8 1/2" x 10 1/2" Bag front and bag back lining
- 2 Sides - Pattern on the CD

Accent Fabric

- 5" x 8 1/2" Inside pocket
- 7" x 8 1/2" Outside pocket lining
- 45" x 1 1/2" Bias – may be pieced

Deco-Magic Lite® or similar product

- 2 - 7 1/2" x 9 1/2" For front and back
- 2 Side interlining pieces – pattern on CD
- 1 - 5 1/2" x 7 1/2" Outside pocket interlining

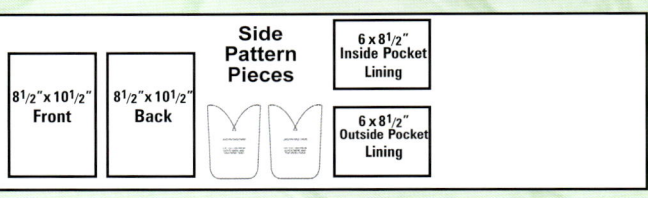

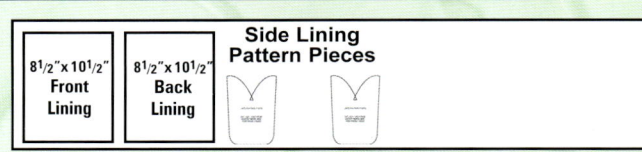

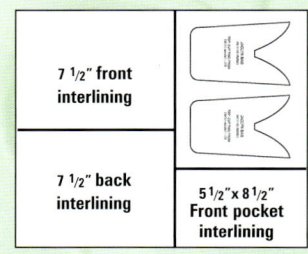

With a Little Help from our Friends

JACLYN'S BAG (CONTINUED)

- Fuse Deco-Magic Lite® to the wrong side of the outside front, back, and sides, leaving 1/2" margin on all sides.

- Fuse Deco-Magic Lite® to the wrong side of the outside pocket leaving 1/2" margin on the sides and the bottom.

- Stitch outside pocket to the outside pocket lining along one of the 8 1/2" edges. Press lining toward seam. Wrap lining over seam allowance and press top edge.

- Top stitch or stitch in the ditch along the binding formed by the pocket lining.

- Stitch inside pocket to the lining in the same manner.

- Draw a line 3" from the bottom of the bag front. Align lower raw edge of the outside pocket with this line. Stitch a 1/2" seam. Trim seam allowance and press pocket toward top.

- On the bottom of the pocket, topstitch 1/4" from the folded edge.

- Baste sides of pocket to the side of the bag.

- Draw a line on the back lining 4 1/2" from the bottom and stitch inside back pocket to back lining in the same manner. Stitch a vertical line in the center of the pocket to create two smaller pockets.

- Stitch bag front and bag back together at the bottom and press seam open.

- Repeat for front and back lining pieces.

With a Little Help from our Friends

JACLYN'S BAG (CONTINUED)

- Cover Micro Welt. See Basic Instructions page 55.

- Mark 1" from the top edge on both sides of the front, back, and covered Micro Welt Cord.

- Stitch Micro Welt Cord on each side of the bag front and back, starting and stopping at the marked line.

- Clip seam allowance of the Micro Welt Cord at the mark and turn cording toward seam allowance.

HINT: To avoid pulling more cording than you wish – pin cord to the project before removing excess cord.

- Use hemostat to remove cording that is turned into seam allowance.

- On each bag side piece, press the 'V' shaped notch to the inside.

- Press the 2" x 8" strap tab fabric in half lengthwise. Open and press raw edges toward center. Press in half creating a strip 1/2" x 8". Stitch closed.

- Cut in half to make two strap tabs. Stitch one of these tabs to each side of the bag 1/2" below the 'V'.

- Turn tabs toward top of bag and topstitch close to fold.

- Pin or Wonder Clip® sides to the front and back. Match center of the sides with the bottom seam of the bag.

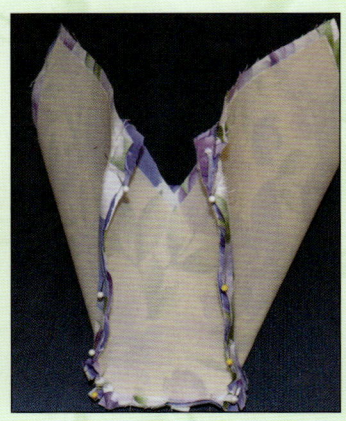

- Align tops of each side to the tops of the front and back.

- Clip curves as needed. The curve is fairly tight so you will need several clips spaced about 1/4" apart. Use your piping foot to stitch and follow the stitching line created from attaching the Micro Welt Cord.

HINT: When sewing a straight edge to a curved edge it is easier if the straight edge is on top.

With a Little Help from our Friends

JACLYN'S BAG   (CONTINUED)

- After sewing both sides to the bag, press seams toward front and back and press under 1/2" along the top openings, curving slightly where sides join to the front and back.

- Stitch lining sides to the front and back lining pieces, starting at the top and stitch ONLY the first 2" of each seam.

- Press seams open.

- Center the zipper tape on each side of the top edges of the lining with the wrong side of the zipper on the right side of the lining. It should extend beyond the opening on each side.

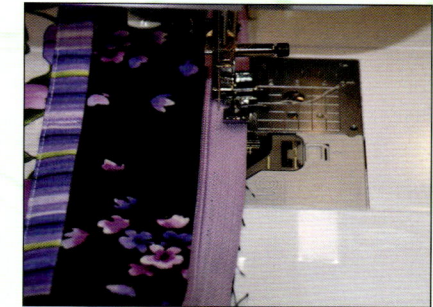

- Stitch each side of the zipper onto the top of the lining starting and stopping at the 'V' on each side.

- Press zipper toward wrong side of lining fabric.

- Marry the zipper together by inserting a zipper pull at each end of zipper.

- Make sure excess zipper is on the wrong side of the lining.

- Stitch across extended ends of zipper tape to ensure the pulls will not come off.

- Complete the construction of the lining following the directions for the outside of the bag.

- Place bag lining inside of the bag itself, wrong sides together.

- Pin together along the zipper edge.

- Top stitch together along the zipper.

- Video also includes an alternate method for attaching the zipper.

115

With a Little Help from our Friends

LEIGH'S YOGA BAG

My friend Leigh has recently become interested in Yoga. She hasn't even purchased a Yoga Mat, but she certainly knows what she would like for her Yoga Bag. The bag features a secure zipper pocket on the outside and plenty of room inside for a mat, towel, water bottle, along with a handy shoulder strap.
And if yoga's not for you, this is a great little Beach Bag!

Supplies

- 30" x 18" Fabric for outside – either a single piece or a combination of fabrics. We used 2 10" x 30" pieces one of which was cut in half and stitched to each long side of the other piece.
- Lining fabric 30"x18" for lining and 12" x 20" for outside zipper pocket.
- 48" of zipper tape with 3 slides.
- 36" of webbing for the strap – will need an additional 10" - 15" plus hardware if you wish the strap to be adjustable. (See page 42 for adjustable strap)
- Wonder Clips
- Seven Corner Ruler®

Fabric provided by Moda Fabrics, Hey Dot by Zen Chic Collection

Construction - All seams are 1/2" unless otherwise noted.

- Use the Seven Corner Ruler® to cut a 3" curve on the top edges of the bag.

- If using more than one fabric, stitch the pieces to form the 30" x 18" outside.

- Follow the directions on page 38 to create the Buttonhole Zipper Pocket centered 1 1/2" from the top of the bag. Zipper box should measure 10" x 1/2".

- Use 11" of Zipper Tape.

With a Little Help from our Friends

LEIGH'S YOGA BAG (CONTINUED)

- With a lengthwise fold, stitch the ends of the bag for 4 1/2" from the fold toward the top of the bag. Clip at the fold and clip to the stitches at the other end of the stitching.

- Repeat for the bag lining.

- Press all seams open.

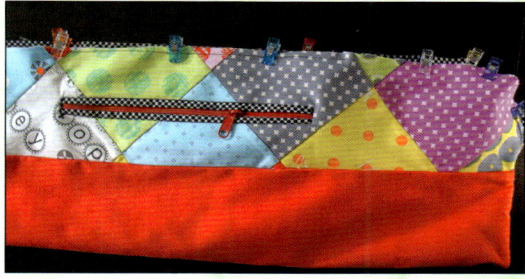

- Insert the lining into the bag, bringing both fabrics to the outside at the clipped seams.

- Separate the zipper tape into two pieces.

- Center one piece to each side of the outside RST, making sure that you have at least 1" of tape extending past the bag opening at each end.

- Serge the edges together. If you do not have a serger, then zig zag stitch the edges together.

- Stitch zipper tape RST to the outside, starting and stopping at the clip points.

- Press zipper to the inside and topstitch at least 1/4" from the fold.

- Attach zipper slide on each end of the zipper.

- Using some fabric scraps, cover the open ends of the zipper to create zipper stops and to finish off the inside of the bag.

LEIGH'S YOGA BAG (CONTINUED)

- Align the raw edge of the strap just below the end of the zipper.
- Stitch across the raw edge.
- Stitch again 1" away from the first stitches.

- Fold the strap back over itself and stitch together.

- From fabric scraps, cut two 1" x 10" strips. Create zipper tabs per directions on page 18.

With a Little Help from our Friends

THE MELINDA BAG

This lovely bag, inspired by Melinda Guistina, is simple to make and yet you can add more variations to make it uniquely yours. The lining has a hidden zipper so there's no need to hand stitch closed! We used a vintage button to accent the front closure, but you can add an optional 3-D embroidery.

Supplies

- 1/2 yd of outer face fabric (ivory embroidered silk)
- 1/2 yd of lining (purple silk)
- 1/2 yd single side Super Shaping Foam® single side fusible
- 1/2 yd of Fantastic Fusible Fabric Backing
- 5/8 yd Micro Welt Cord
- 2 Tube Turners : sizes 2 & 4
- Vintage or decorative button
- Pattern printed from CD
- Optional embroidery: polyester or nylon organdy & matching thread
- 10" Zipper tape & 1 slide
- 60" Purse chain with 2 D-rings
- Basting tape
- Wonder Clips
- Zipper foot and or piping foot

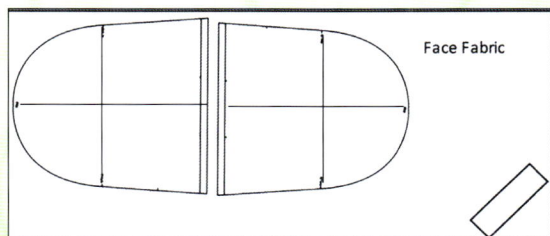
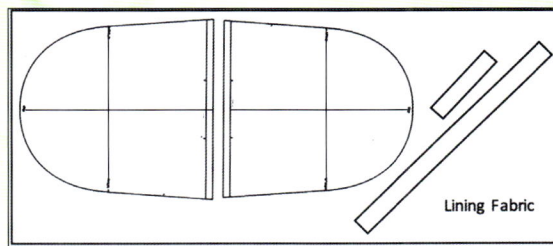

Cutting

Face Fabric
- Print and cut out pattern from the CD. Cut 2 patterns of face fabric.
- 1 - 2" x 6" on the bias for D-ring strap loops

Super Shaping Foam®
- 2 of the pattern

Lining
- 2 of the pattern. After you cut out your pattern, trim 1/2" off the bottom to make it 1/2" shorter then the bag outside.
- 1 - 1" x 6" for button loop
- 1 - 1 1/2" x 22" for piping

With a Little Help from our Friends

THE MELINDA BAG (CONTINUED)

Construction
Face Fabric

- Fuse shaping foam to the wrong side of face fabric.
- Sew face fabric sections together at the bottom edge.
- Press seam open.
- Mark with a pin 1 1/4" from the center seam toward the rounded end. Pleat the fabric by bringing the pin to the seam.
- Mark with a pin on the sides and notch the fabric as indicated on the pattern.

- Pleat the bottom and pin in place with wonder clips.
- Sew from the bottom pleat up to the notch, as indicated on the pattern.

Button Loop

- Take button loop piece and fold in half lengthwise and sew with 1/4" seam allowance. Using Tube Turner size 2, turn right side out. (You may need to adjust the length of this depending on the button you chose.)
- Fold the loop in half and sew at the top center.

Micro Welt Trim

- Using bias, make Micro Welt Piping and sew along flap edge. (See page 55.)
- To sew trim to top edge of bag, trim away 1/2" of cord at the starting end so that you can fold back your fabric for a finished end. Sew onto the same side where you sewed your button loop.

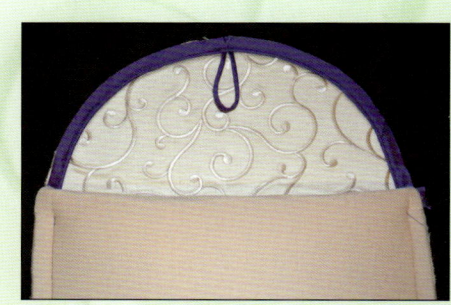

With a Little Help from our Friends

THE MELINDA BAG   (CONTINUED)

Micro Welt Trim (CONTINUED)

- End your trim in the same way, by trimming away cord and folding fabric end under.

Strap Loops

- To make strap loops, sew your 2" strip with a 1/2" seam allowance, and turn right side out using tube turner size 4.

- Cut into 2" lengths. Fold in half through D-rings and sew along sides just above the notch where the stitching ends.

Lining

- Cut two of lining and Fantastic Fusible Fabric Backing.
- Fuse fabric backing to the wrong side of lining.

- To insert a zipper in the lining, please refer to page 19.
- Sew the lining bottom by pleating in the same manner.
- Sew the sides up to the notch as indicated by the pattern.
- Turn the lining right side out and pin the lining to the face fabric.

Finishing

- With your lining right side out and your bag inside out, pin the top curved edges together by starting at the center top.

With a Little Help from our Friends

THE MELINDA BAG (CONTINUED)

Finishing (CONTINUED)

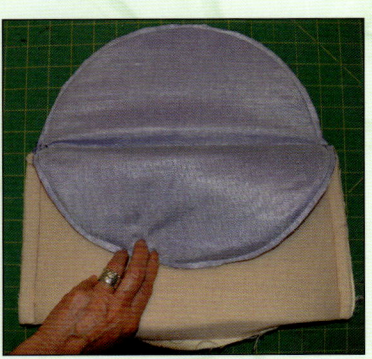

- Sew top curves on both sides.
- Once the top is sewn, open the bottom zipper and turn the bag right side out by pulling through the opening in the lining.

Zip Closed

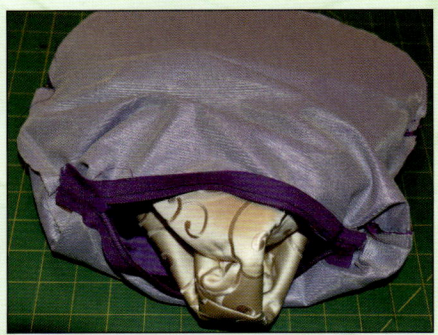

- Fold over flap and sew on decorative or fabric covered button in line with the button loop.

OPTIONAL: *For a variation try adding some 3-D embroidery on the fold over flap!*

With a Little Help from our Friends

TEACHER'S PET

This bag was inspired by Penny Pombrio, a Junior High School Technology teacher. She wanted a bag big enough to carry her personal effects, as well as everything she needed for work. She wanted an inner pocket to carry a laptop or tablet that was, as she put it, "Not floppy". There's an inside zipper pocket, and two outside pockets, but as with all the bags in this book, you can add or delete features to suit your own needs. I used 4 different quilt weight fabrics because it was what I had, so feel free to use more or less patterns, based on your stash.

Supplies
- 5/8 yd Cuddle Suede
- 5/8 yd Lining fabric (pale pink)
- 1 Fat quarter accent fabric #1 (black)
- 1 Fat quarter accent fabric #2 (pink print)
- 1/2 yd Large motif print for pocket
- 5 3/4 yds of Micro Welt for piping
- Lame Stylo thread for embroidery
- 7/8 yd Décor Bond 15 1/2" x 20", 2 - 8 1/2" squares
- 1 package Sew Fab Foam® Single Sided Fusible
- 1 3/4 yd zipper tape with 6 slides (Cut 2 - 8 1/2", 1 - 20", 1 - 15", and 1 - 7 1/2")
- Basting tape
- Optional: Permanent Double Stick Tape
- Deco-Magic® cut 1" x 94" (you will have to join two pieces to get this length)

Cuddle Suede fabric provided by Shannon Fabrics

Cutting Layout (All diagrams below are single thickness)

Bag Outside

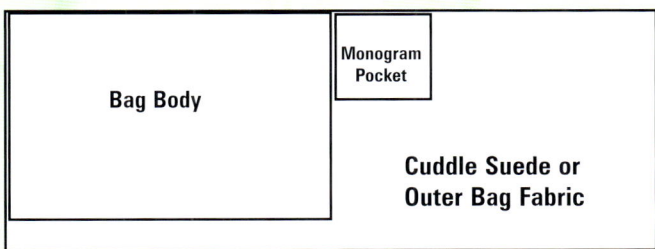

1 - 20" x 30"; 1- 8 1/2" square

Lining #1

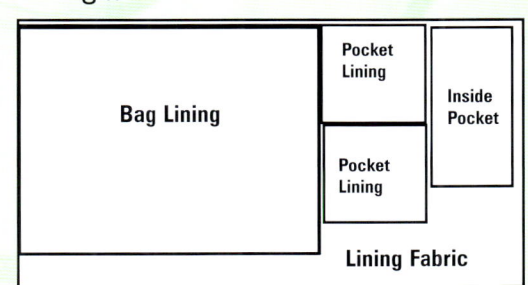

1- 20" x 25"; 1-7 1/2" x 14"; 2- 8 1/2" square

123

TEACHER'S PET (CONTINUED)

Cutting Layout (CONTINUED)

Decor Bond

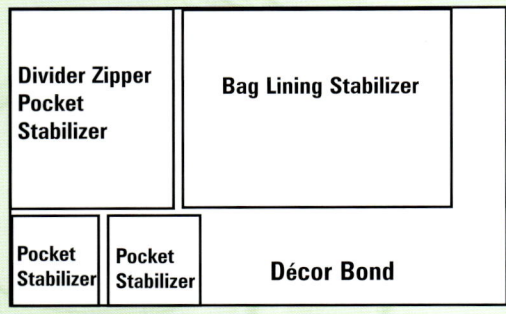

1- 20" x 25"; 1- 19" x 15"; 2- 8 ½" squares

Accent #1

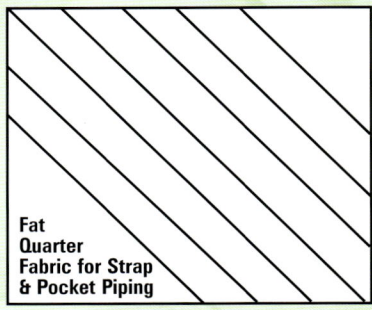

120" of 2 ½" bias (See page 10.)

Accent #2

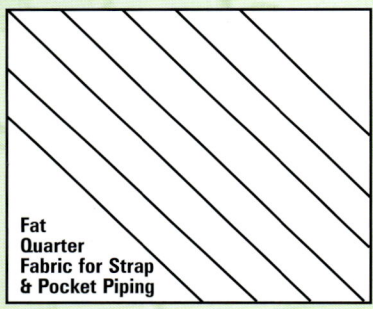

100" of 2" bias (See page 10.)

Large Motif Print

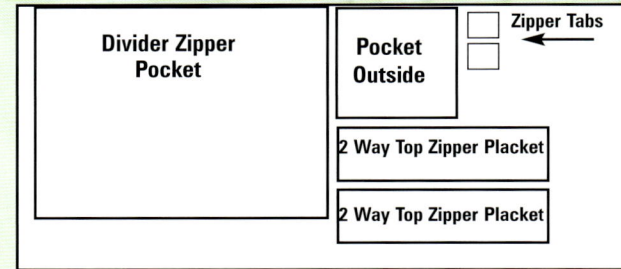

1- 8 ½" square; 1 – 20" x 15"; 2 – 5" x 15"; 2- 2" squares

Construction - All seam allowances are ½" unless otherwise indicated

Bag Body

- Start by fusing the bag body to a 20" x 30" piece of Sew Fab® Foam.

- Mark the center of each side edge to indicate where the center bottom will be.

- To make the Round Box Corner, use the Seven Corner Ruler® and cut with a rotary cutter.

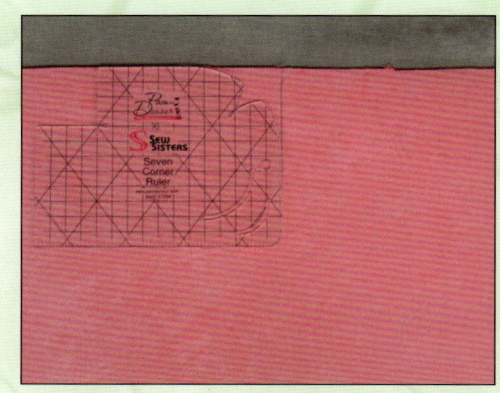

With a Little Help from our Friends

TEACHER'S PET (CONTINUED)

Construction (CONTINUED)

Bag Body (CONTINUED)

- To make a Rounded Box Corner, use the notched curved corner on the Seven Corner Ruler®, or mark your corner with your favorite ruler. (See page 27 for Rounded Box Corners.)

- Both sides will look like this.

The Outside Pockets

- Add Décor Bond to the two 8 $1/2$" outside pockets to stabilize.

- If you choose to add the optional monogram, add embroidery onto one pocket. (See embroidery page 9.)

- Add Micro Welt to the top edge as shown, with raw edges together. (Make Micro Welt from the 2 $1/2$" bias. See page 55 for Welt Cord and Micro Welt).

- Sew lining fabric onto your pocket pieces, with right sides together, at the top and bottom edges only, leaving the sides open.

- Turn right side out and press flat.

- To add a zipper, as we did on the monogramed pocket, cut a zipper the width of the pocket.

- Fold a 2" wide strip of bias in half lengthwise and press.

- Sew raw edges of the bias to one side of zipper tape with a $1/4$" SA and cut to the width of the pocket.

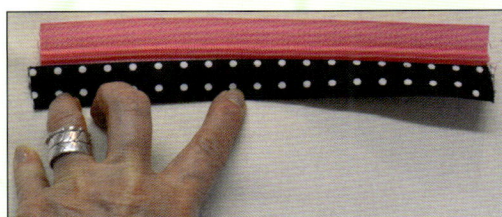

- Fold back and press flat, with the folded edge to the outside.

With a Little Help from our Friends

TEACHER'S PET (CONTINUED)

Construction (CONTINUED)

The Outside Pockets (CONTINUED)

- Place the other side of the zipper tape to the back top edge of the momogramed pocket and stitch in the ditch of the piping.

- Center both pockets, on each side of your bag, with the top edges 4" from the center of the bag.

- Pin in place and topstitch along the bottom of both pockets. Top stitch the top edge (the banding) of the Monogram Pocket.

The Straps

Although this bag appears to have two straps, the strap is actually all one continuous piece that is 92" long.

- To make the strap for this bag, make it one continuous piece that is 92" long. Splice by folding at an angle, press, and sew in the crease line.

- For directions on piped straps, please refer to page 43.

- After the strap is made, attach to the bag.

- First, divide the strap in half, mark with pins, then mark the bottom center of the bag and pin your strap, lining up the pins 5 3/4" from the side edges, covering the pocket edges.

- Stitch in the ditch of the piping on each strap, stopping at the top edges of your outer pockets. Reinforce the stitching at the top of each strap.

TEACHER'S PET (CONTINUED)

Construction (CONTINUED)

Side Seams

- Sew the "V" at each corner, tapering as you would if making a dart.

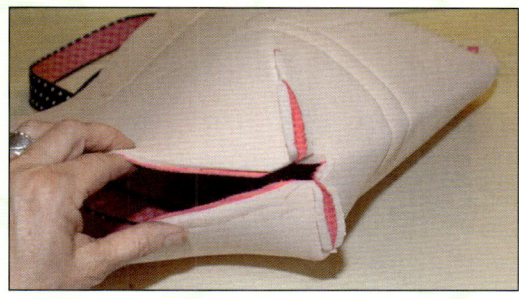

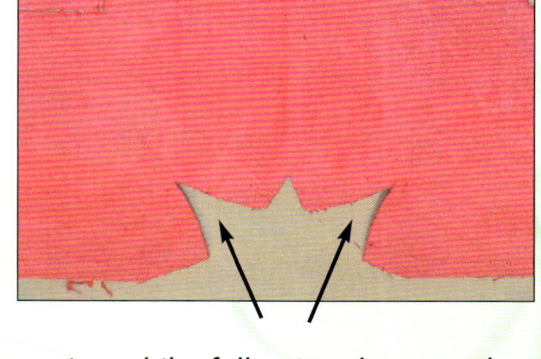

- With the "V" seams pinned open, sew the sides seams all the way down, curving while following the cut edge, tapering at the bottom.

Bag Lining

- Fuse Décor Bond to the wrong side of the bag lining.

- If wish to put an inside pocket as we did here, draw a zipper box on the wrong side of the inside zipper pocket fabric.

- The box will be $1/2$" by $5\ 1/2$", with $1\ 1/2$" at the top and 1" at each side.

- Place on your lining fabric, with the top edge of the pocket $3\ 1/2$" from the top edge of the bag lining.

- Starting on one long side of the drawn zipper box, sew all the way around. Do not stitch past your line and do not back stitch. If you do, rip it out and re-sew. (See page 38.)

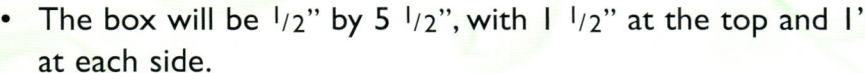

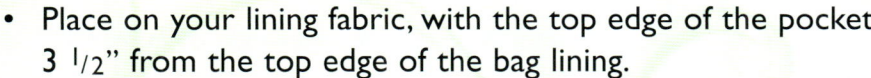

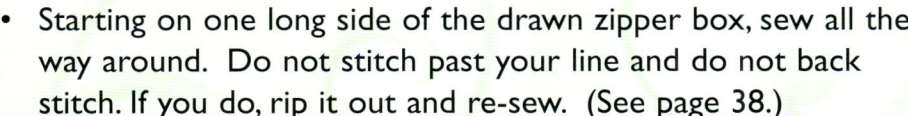

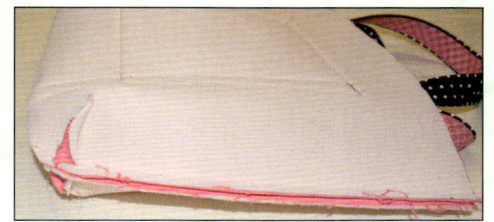

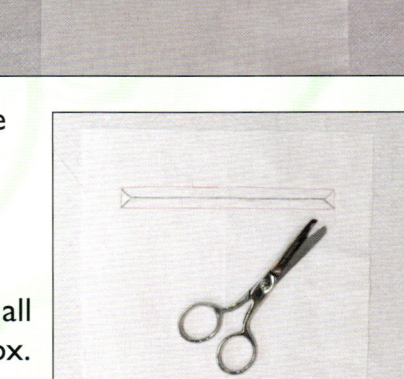

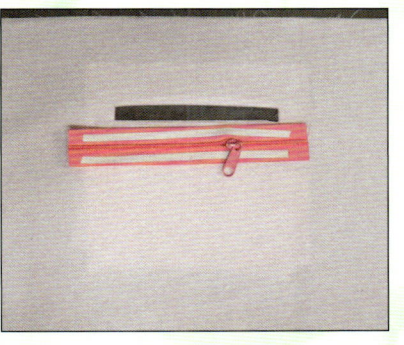

- Cut down the center of the box, making a "Y" at each end, cutting all the way into the corner of the box.

- Pull the fabric through to the back, and press flat.

- Cut a 7" section of zipper tape, and install slide. Apply basting tape to each side.

TEACHER'S PET (CONTINUED)

Construction (CONTINUED)

Bag Lining

- Center zipper in opening and edge stitch all the way around.

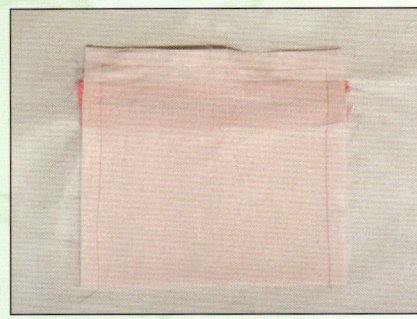

- Fold the pocket up in half, and sew the two sides and the top.

- Mark the center of the bottom of the lining by drawing a line on the wrong side, from side to side.

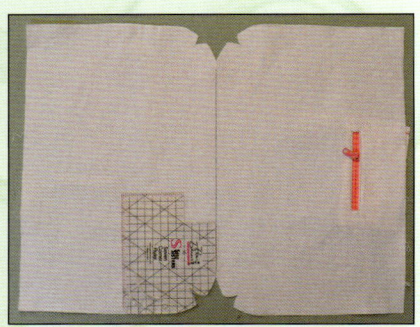

- Using the Seven Corner Ruler®, cut your corners to match your bag outside.

- Sew the "V" at each corner, tapering as you would if making a dart, like you did for the bag outside.

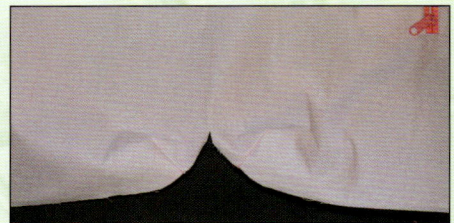

Dividing Zipper Pocket

- To make this pocket, please turn to page 40 for complete instructions.

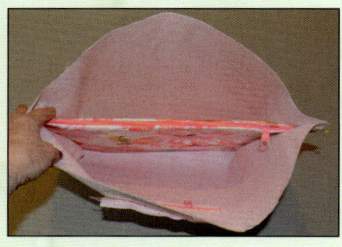

- Insert your Dividing Zipper Pocket in between the two sides of your bag lining, with the zipper edge of the pocket 2" below the top edge of the lining. Make the bottom edge of the dividing pocket follow the curve of the bottom of lining.

- Sew sides with a $1/2$" SA.

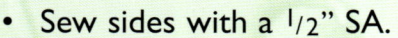

NOTE: The dividing pocket is narrower than the bag, and this is what pulls the ends in and gives the bag its shape.

TEACHER'S PET (CONTINUED)

Construction (CONTINUED)

Two-Way Top Zipper Placket

- Please turn to page 23 for complete instructions on how to make this placket.

- After you make your Two-Way Top Zipper Tab, pin it to the top edge of bag, with RST.

- Baste in place.

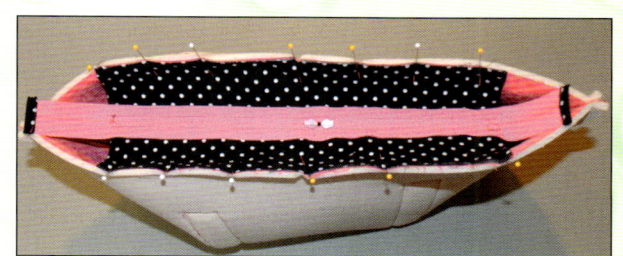

Bag Assembly

- Once your lining and outer layers are finished, it's time to sew it together!

- With RST, match the lining to the bag outside, and match at the seams.

- Using Wonder Clips or pins to hold in place, sew along the top edge, leaving a 10" opening to turn the bag right side out along one side. Back stitch both ends of your stitching.

- Once the bag is turned right side out, use Permanent Double Stick Tape or hand stitch to close opening.

- Push the bag lining down to the bottom of the bag. This will make the outside fabric roll to the inside.

- Press down to crease the outer fabric.

Sew on the Go

Sew on the Go

ESSENTIAL TRAVEL & COSMETIC BAGS

These bags may be my favorite ones in the book. The travel bag can easily hold full size products for your hair and other grooming needs. The cosmetic bag 'Holds Everything' you need and easily packs inside of the travel bag!

NOTE: *The supplies and cutting instructions for each bag will be listed first, followed by construction directions which are identical for each bag.*

Essential Travel Bag
Supplies
- ¾ yd Outside fabric
- ¾ yd Inside fabric
- 18" x 58" package Super Shaping Foam® Double Sided Fusible
- 9" x 11" piece Deco Magic® or similar stabilizer.
- One fat quarter of accent fabric
- 30" Zipper Tape with 2 slides
- 2 ¼" yds Micro Welt Cord
- Wonder Clips

Cutting Instructions
Cut and label all pieces.

- Cut an 11" x WOF piece of both the inside and outside fabric. Fuse these to a piece of the Super Shaping Foam® and quilt. (See page 38.)

2 ½" x 28 ¼" Top Band	10" x 12" Top
6" x 28 ¼" Bottom Band	

- From this quilted fabric, cut the top and bottom bands and bag top as pictured.

- From the outside fabric, cut a 14 ½" x 4" bag handle.

- Cut a 9" square from the inside fabric, outside fabric and Super Shaping Foam®. Fuse and quilt.

- From this quilted piece, cut the 7 ½" x 8" center back.

7 ½" x 8" Center Back

- From the inside fabric, cut a 10" x 12" bag bottom.

Sew on the Go

ESSENTIAL TRAVEL & COSMETIC BAGS

Essential Travel Bag

Cutting Instructions (CONTINUED)
Cut and label all pieces.

- Cut 11" x 13" pieces of outside fabric and Super Shaping Foam® and fuse fabric to one side of the Super Shaping Foam®. **You will need to use a Pressing Sheet on the other side of the foam to keep it from fusing to the ironing board.** Quilt.

- From this piece, cut a 10" x 12" bottom.

- Use the 3" curve on the Seven Corner Ruler® to shape the four corners of the bag bottom, bag top, inside bag bottom and the 9" x 11" piece of Deco-Magic®.

10" x 12" Bottom

Essential Cosmetic Bag

Supplies

- 3/8 yd Outside fabric
- 3/8 yd Inside fabric
- 15" x 45" piece of Super Shaping Foam® Double Sided Fusible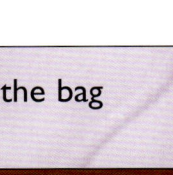
- 5" x 8" piece Deco-Magic® or similar stabilizer. (Use pattern piece from the CD to shape.)
- One fat quarter of accent fabric
- 18" Zipper tape with 2 slides
- 1 1/2 yds Micro Welt Cord

Cutting Instructions - *Cut and label all pieces.*

- Cut a 7" x WOF piece of both the inside and outside fabric. Fuse these to a piece of the Super Shaping Foam® and quilt.

- From this quilted fabric, cut the top and bottom bands, center back and bag top as pictured.

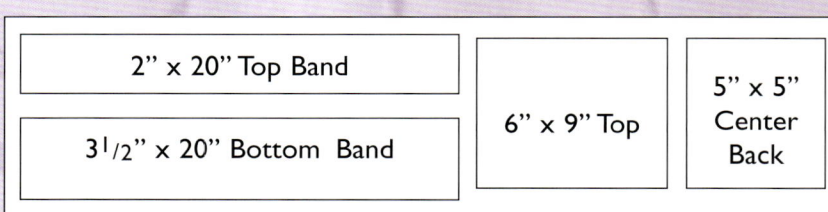

2" x 20" Top Band
3 1/2" x 20" Bottom Band
6" x 9" Top
5" x 5" Center Back

Sew on the Go

ESSENTIAL TRAVEL & COSMETIC BAGS (CONTINUED)

Essential Cosmetic Bag

Cutting Instructions (CONTINUED)

- From the outside fabric cut a 10" x 4" bag handle.

- From the inside fabric cut a 6" x 9'" bag bottom.

- Cut 7" x 10" pieces of outside fabric and Super Shaping Foam® and fuse fabric to one side of the Super Shaping Foam®. **You will need to use a Pressing Sheet on the other side of the foam to keep it from fusing to the ironing board. Quilt.**

- From this piece, cut a 6" x 9" bottom.

- Use the pattern piece included on the CD to shape the bag bottom, bag top and inside bag bottom.

Construction for both
The Travel Bag & The Cosmetic Bag

All Seams are 1/2" unless otherwise noted.

- Follow direction on page 10 to create bias fabric. Follow only the first step to create a parallelogram.

- Because you will need bias fabric in three different widths, it will be easier to cut those strips from this parallelogram shaped fabric and join them into the needed lengths for trim, welt and binding.

- **Zipper Trim** – For the Travel Bag, cut enough strips at 2" wide to generate 60" in length. (40" for the cosmetic Bag)

- **Micro Welt** – For the Travel Bag, cut strips 1 1/2" wide and create 75" of length. (50" long for cosmetic bag).

- **Binding** – all remaining bias should be cut at 2 1/2" wide and joined to use to bind interior bag seams.

- Follow directions on page 54 to create the Zipper Trim and insert the zipper between the top and bottom bands.

ESSENTIAL TRAVEL & COSMETIC BAGS (CONTINUED)

Construction for Both Bags (CONTINUED)

NOTE: The inside fabric on our sample is a directional fabric. If you choose something like this, be careful to keep the print running in the right direction when you do this step!

- Attach a zipper slide on each end of the zipper.

- Stitch short edges of the completed band to each side of the center back piece.

- If the band does not quite match with the height of the center back, trim the longer of the two to make them even.

- Trim the seam allowances to ¼" and use the 2 ½" binding to cover and encase seam allowance. See page 49 for detailed instructions on French Binding the seams.

- Follow directions on page 55 to cover the Micro Welt Cord.

- Attached finished Micro Welt to the top and bottom edges of the completed band. Follow Welt Cord directions for joining the cord.

NOTE: If you use a different color thread in the bobbin it will be easier to see when you need to stitch on top of it in the following steps.

- Fuse the trimmed piece of Deco Magic® to the wrong side of the piece of inside fabric you cut for the bag bottom.

Sew on the Go

ESSENTIAL TRAVEL & COSMETIC BAGS (CONTINUED)

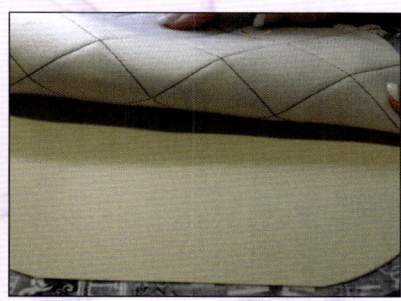

Construction for Both Bags (CONTINUED)

- Layer both bottom pieces WST and stitch with a scant $1/2$" seam.
- Use pins to divide the band and the bag bottom into quarters.
- Pin or clip together, centering the center back on one of the long sides of the bottom.

NOTE: Wonder Clips® are very helpful for holding these pieces together for stitching.

- Use a piping foot to stitch with the band on top and the bag bottom piece underneath, clipping the curves as necessary. You should be stitching on top of or just to the left of the stitches used to attach the Micro Welt to the band.

- Check to see that the welt is properly encased in the seam.

- Trim seam allowance to $1/4$" and bind seam to create a finished edge. See binding directions on page 49.

- Create the handle for the top of the bag.

- Press the handle piece in half lengthwise.

- Cut a strip of Super Shaping Foam® 1" by the length of the handle. Align this with the inside fold and fuse to the wrong side of the handle piece.

- Press the long raw edges of the handle to the center fold.

- Fold together and topstitch close to each edge.

- Center handle ends on the short sides of the top and stitch a box to secure.

- Stitch bag top to the band in the same manner as the bag bottom.

- Trim and bind the seam allowance as you did for the bag bottom.

- From fabric scraps, cut two 1" x 9" strips. Create Zipper Tabs following directions on page 18.

135

Sew on the Go

TRAVEL ROLL UP

This little roll up will hold all of your essentials for that quick get away! The bottom pockets are divided for your jewelry, while the remaining pockets are perfect for travel size cosmetics and personal care items.

Supplies

- 1/3 yd each outside fabric, inside fabric, clear vinyl
- 10" x 30" piece of batting
- 2 yds of zipper tape and 7 slides
- Decorative thread
- 1 1/4 yd narrow ribbon for ties (may use leftover outside fabric to stitch the ties using the instructions for Zipper Tabs on page 18.)
- 1/8 yd coordinating fabric for binding.
- Wonder Clips

Construction

- Cut outside fabric, inside fabric and clear vinyl into 10" x 30" pieces.

- Use the diagram to the right to mark pocket lines on the vinyl.
  (Sharpie® marker works well.)

- 5"-	- 5"-	- 5"-	- 5"-	- 2"-	- 3"-	- 4"-

- Cut the zipper tape into seven 10" pieces.

- Thread machine with decorative thread and have some fun selecting a different decorative stitch for each piece of the zipper tape. 5-7mm wide stitches work best. Use an open toe foot or the standard foot that came with your machine. If the stitch opening on the foot extends beyond the width of the zipper tape, you will have to narrow the width of the stitch to insure that you do not stitch off of the tape. You might also want to look at lengthening some of the stitches.

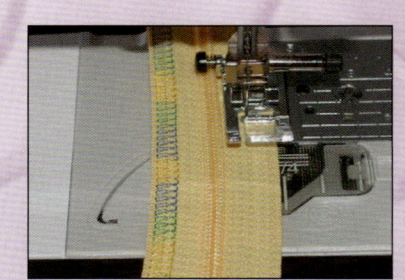

Sew on the Go

TRAVEL ROLL UP (CONTINUED)

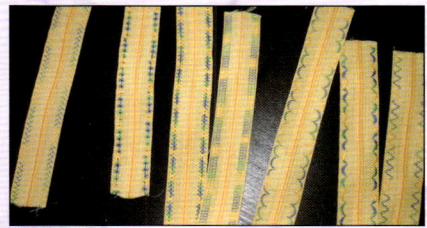

- Turn the vinyl piece so it is 10" wide and 30" long with the 4" mark toward the bottom.

- The top piece of zipper tape should be placed 1/2" from the top cut edge.

- Stitch ONLY the LOWER EDGE of the zipper tape to the vinyl, using thread that closely matches the zipper tape and stitch close to the bottom edge of the tape so that you maintain the effect of your decorative stitches.

- For the remaining 6 pieces of zipper tape, align the top of the tape with your marked lines and again stitch ONLY the LOWER EDGE of the zipper tape to the vinyl.

- Sandwich the outside fabric, batting and inside fabric, pin or Wonder Clip along the edges.

- Add the vinyl piece on top of the inside fabric and pin or clip only to the top edge.

- Beginning with the top zipper, stitch ONLY THE UPPER EDGE of the zipper tape through all layers, again using thread that closely matches the zipper tape and stitch close to the edge of the tape.

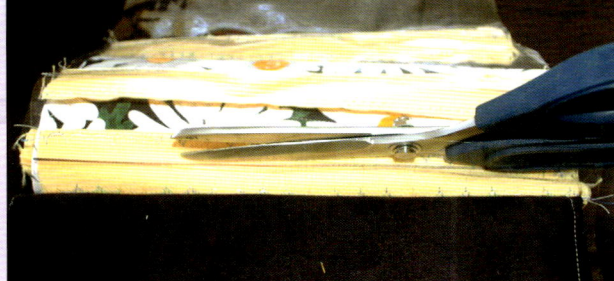

- Flip the vinyl piece to the wrong side and trim the vinyl from behind the zipper teeth.

- Repeat for the remaining 6 pieces of zipper tape, stitch ONLY THE UPPER EDGES and trimming the vinyl from behind the zipper teeth as you stitch each one.

- Stitch a vertical line in the middle of the bottom pocket, creating two smaller pockets perfect for bracelets!

Sew on the Go

TRAVEL ROLL UP (CONTINUED)

- Divide the next pocket into 3 equal sections. These are perfect for earrings!

- The narrow 2" pocket is for necklaces or bracelets.

- Attach a zipper slide to each zipper.

- Stitch all layers together close to the outside edges.

- Cut 5" of the ribbon to form a hanging loop. Cut the remaining ribbon into 2 equal pieces for ties.

- Pin the loop to the top of the outside, spreading the two edges 1" apart.

- Pin the ties in the center of the loop.

- Stitch across all pieces of ribbon at 1/4" from the edge.

- From the coordinating fabric, cut two strips 2 1/4" x WOF and piece together for the binding.

- Press binding in half and apply in your preferred manner. For this project, I chose to stitch it first on the vinyl side and topstitch it on the outside using a zig zag stitch. This is also another opportunity to use a decorative stitch!

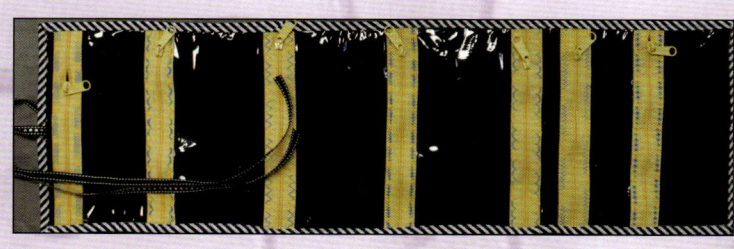

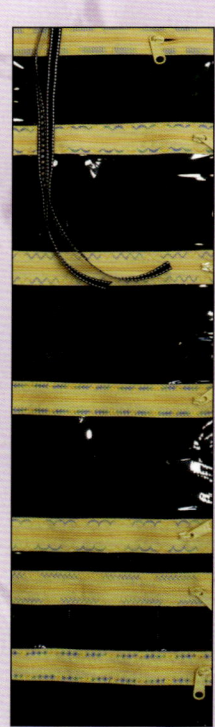

Sew on the Go

GRAB-N-GO MAKE UP BAG

This mini bag is small enough to go into any purse and will hold essentials such as make-up, pens, or other small items that need be kept together. If this bag isn't the right size for you, take your print-out pattern to your copier and resize to suit your needs. (Check out our Proportional Scale at www.pamdmour.com)

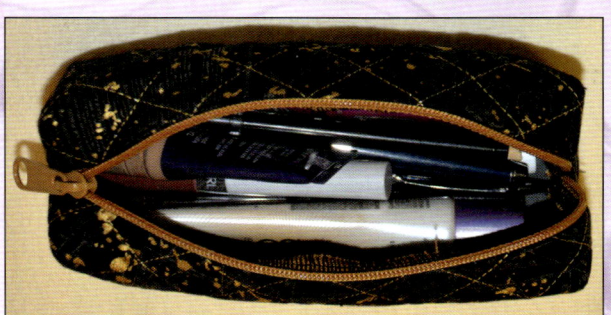

I prefer to make this entire bag with the serger. If your serger has a chain stitch, you can also quilt this on the serger.

Supplies

- 2- 10" layer cake squares
- 1 - 10" square batting, or Super Shaping Foam®, double sided
- 10" zipper with slide
- Decorative thread for quilting
- Matching thread for sewing
- Pattern printed out from book CD

GRAB & GO MAKE UP BAG

CUT 2 TO MAKE ONE WHOLE PATTERN

CUT TWO OF PATTERN

CUT ONE OF SUPER SHAPING FOAM

Join this side

Construction

- Make your quilt "sandwich" by layering your outer fabric, batting and inner fabric and fuse.

- Mark and quilt fabric using directions on page 50, or use your own decorative stitches or pattern.

- Print out your pattern from the book CD and cut out your quilted fabric.

- Separate your zipper and sew one piece to each long side with right sides together.

Fabric provided by Moda Fabrics, Modern Background Luster by Zen Chic Collection

139

Sew on the Go

GRAB-N-GO MAKE UP BAG (CONTINUED)

Construction (CONTINUED)

- Once your zipper slide is on, zip all the way off, open one end back up about 2-3" and re-insert slide. Leave it in the center so that both ends of the zipper are sealed like this.

- This technique makes it much easier to sew across the ends!

- Sew across ends. If using a regular sewing machine, finish seam with a zig-zag or seam overcast stitch.

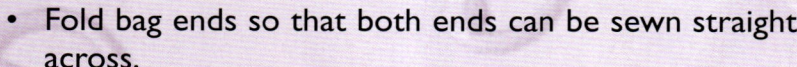

- Fold bag ends so that both ends can be sewn straight across.

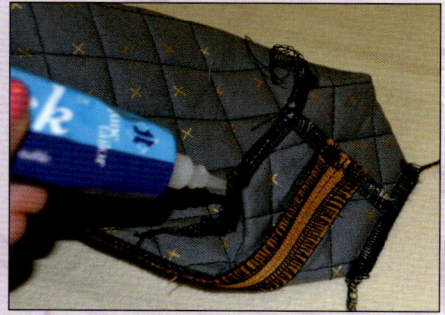

- Add a small amount of Fray Block to keep fabic from fraying at the corners.

- Turn right side out and enjoy your new bag!

Fabric provided by Maywood Studios, Catalina Ultra Violet Collection

Sew on the Go

MEN'S TOILETRY BAG

To make this large men's travel bag to hold all their travel toiletries, follow the instructions from the Essential Mini Bag, but print out the larger pattern.

Supplies

- 2 Fat quarters
- 1 piece of Super Shaping Foam® double sided, 19" x 15"
- 20" of zipper tape with slide
- Decorative thread
- Matching thread
- Carry strap: 1 piece of bias 1 ½" x 8"
- Carry strap: 1 piece of fusible stabilizer (We use Deco-Magic™ Lite) ¾" x 7"
- Optional: laminating vinyl

NOTE: *If you choose to make a waterproof lining for your bag, use Single Sided Super Shaping Foam®, quilt the outside fabric only, then laminate your lining according the the instructions on page 52 or 53.*

Construction

- Assemble using Essential Mini Bag instructions, with this one exception: this bag has a carry strap at one end.

- Carry strap: fuse stabilizer to the wrong side of bias strip.

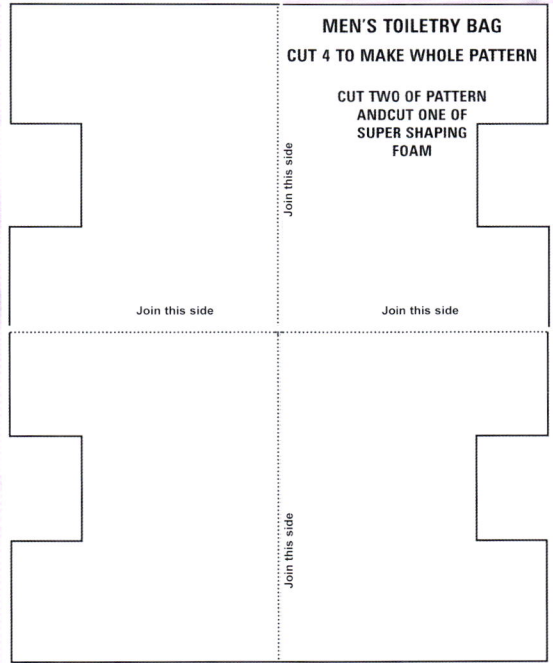

Option #1

- Use a ¾" belt loop maker, with your serger set for wide cover stitch, with the right side up as shown.

Sew on the Go

MEN'S TOILETRY BAG   (CONTINUED)

Construction   (CONTINUED)

Option #2

- Another option to a serger cover stitch is to use a 6mm twin need on your sewing machine and thread both needles.

- Press fabric over stabilizer.

- Center under foot with folded edges down and sew with twin needle.

- Before sewing ends, tuck the strap into one end of the bag, with the raw edges lined up as shown.

- After tabs are in place, sew end seam.

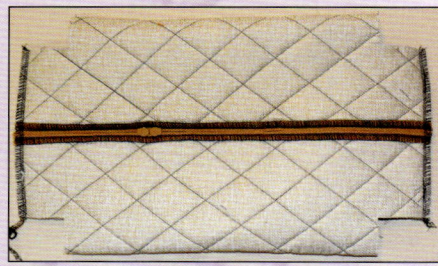

- Sew corners. If you have a serger, use a 4 thread overlock. Otherwise, use your sewing machine and finish seams with a zig-zag.

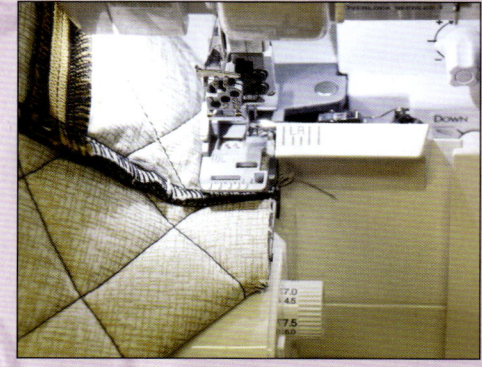

Sew on the Go

WATER TOTE

Everywhere we go we see people toting around a bottle of water. Why not make a classy carrier for that bottle? And this one is not only classy, it is also very practical. Made of neoprene, it will help insulate the bottle, and it features an outside pocket as well.

Supplies and Cutting: This is a great 'stash' project!

Outside Fabric: - neoprene or fabric quilted with Super Shaping Foam®

- 5" circle for the base (pattern is on CD)
- 6" x 13 1/2" Lower portion - neoprene or quilted with Super Shaping Foam®

Outside Top Fabric

- 3 1/2" x 13 1/2" - fabric you create with precuts (see page 155) or a single piece of fabric.

Lining Fabric:

- 5" circle for the base (laminated) (pattern is on CD)
- 4" x 12 1/2" pocket lining
- 8" x 13 1/2" inside lining (laminated)
- 4" x 13 1/2" drawstring band
- 1" x 24" drawstring
- 2 pieces 2" x 6" to bind pocket sides

Pocket Front:

- 4" x 5 1/2" outer pocket piece - from a fabric that coordinates with the others

Notions:

- 40" strapping 3/4" - 1" wide
- D-ring
- Strap Adjuster
- Cord Stop
- 3/8 yd Heat 'n Bond Iron-Vinyl
- 4" circle Deco-Magic® to stabilize the base of the lining. (pattern is on CD)

Fabric provided by Maywood Studios Catalina Ultraviolet Collection

Sew on the Go

WATER TOTE (CONTINUED)

Construction - *All seams are 1/2" unless otherwise noted.*

- Stitch pocket lining to top edge of pocket RST.

- Press lining up and over the seam allowance to create a binding.

- At the bottom of the outside, fold the lining up with RST to create the pocket. The back of the pocket should extend 1" above the top of the binding.

- Baste sides close to the edge.

- Press the 2" x 6" binding strips in half WST.

- Using the French Binding Method on page 49, stitch one strip to each side of the pocket with a 1/4" seam allowance.

NOTE: If using Neoprene, you will need to stitch all seams with tear away stabilizer.

- Fold and press binding strips to the inside of the pocket piece, making sure the binding extends past the stitching on the back.

- Center the pocket on the bottom section of the bag and stitch in the ditch along the binding seam.

- Stitch the upper bag to the lower portion.

- Stitch the side seam.

- Divide the bag bottom and the bottom edge of the bag into quarters.

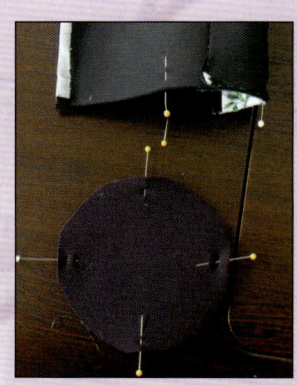

Sew on the Go

WATER TOTE (CONTINUED)

- Align these marks to attach the body of the bag to the bag bottom.

- Stitch.

- Trim bottom seam allowance to $1/4$".

- Turn bag right side out.

- Attach Strap Adjuster to one end of the bag strap.

- Slide D-ring onto strap.

- Feed open end of the strap through the adjuster.

- Cut 4" of strapping and slide through the D-ring.

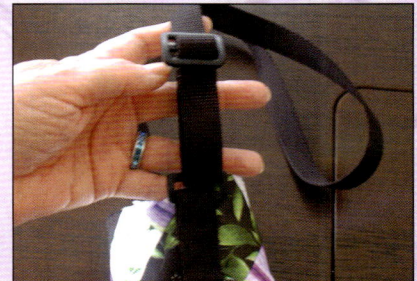

- Fold this piece of strap to hide the two raw edges and stitch to one side of the bag.

- Fold raw edge of the other end of the strap to the inside and stitch to the other side of the bag.

Sew on the Go

WATER TOTE (CONTINUED)

- Fuse 4" circle of Deco-Magic® to the lining bottom.
- Stitch lining side seam.
- Stitch lining to lining bottom, quartering as you did for the outside of the bag.
- Trim seam to $1/4$".
- Insert lining into the bag.

NOTE: If the free arm on your machine is too large to use, the next steps will be much easier if you turn the bag inside out.

- Stitch outside and lining together close to the top edge.

- Stitch side seam of the drawstring band, leaving a 1" opening $1/4$" from one end.

- Fold band in half WST.

- Align band to top of bag, making sure the opening on the band is facing the outside of the bag.

- Stitch to bag top with a $1/4$" seam allowance.

- Fold band to inside covering seam allowance and topstitch on the outside.

- To create drawstring, follow directions on page 18 for Zipper Tabs.

- Insert drawstring through the band. Attach cord stop and tie raw edges in a knot.

Quick Projects using Pre-Cuts

Quick Projects using Pre-Cuts

WRISTLET KEY CHAIN

This is a super quick and easy project you can make using leftover zipper tape and leftover fabric. If you wish to use pre-cuts, one Layer Cake will yield 2 key chains or one lanyard.

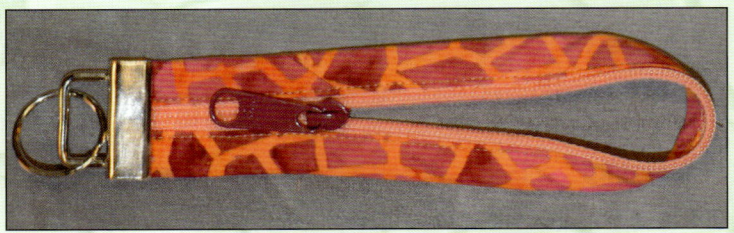

NOTE: If using a Layer Cake and you are only making one key chain, you can cut one on the bias without seams.

Supplies
- 1 Layer Cake pre-cuts or fabric scraps
- 1 Single side of zipper tape 12" long
- 1 Zipper slide
- 1 Set key chain hardware
- 1/4" Basting tape
- Zipper foot

Fabric provided by Moda Fabrics, Batiks by Moda Collection

Construction
- Make a parallelogram from your 10" square. (See page 10 for more instructions.) This is sewing the two straight grain edges together. Press seam open. Cut two strips 2 1/4" wide. From the remaining fabric, cut 2 - 2 1/4" squares for tabs.

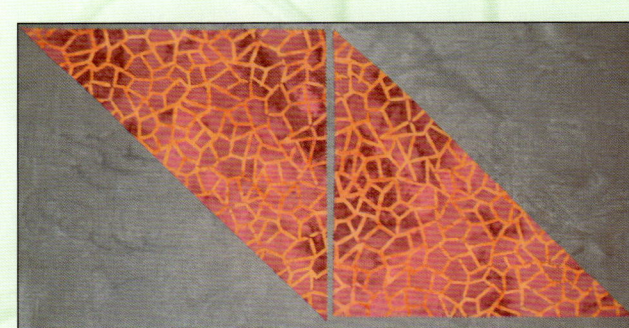

- If you only want to make one key chain, cut your 2 1/4" strip down the center, as shown, and cut one 2 1/2" square for the tab.

- Begin by sewing the WRONG side of the zipper to the RIGHT side of the fabric with raw edges together. (Zipper teeth will be up.)

Quick Projects using Pre-cuts

WRISTLET KEY CHAIN (CONTINUED)

Construction (CONTINUED)

- Add basting tape to the right side of fabric opposite the edge of the zipper tape.

- Fold over the raw edge that has the basting tape. Line up fold near, but not touching, the zipper teeth. Stitch along folded edge.

- Marry the ends of the zipper with the slide.

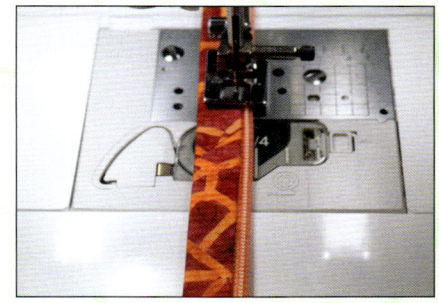

Adding the Tab

- Sew the right side of the tab fabric to the wrong side of key chain with a ¼" seam allowance.

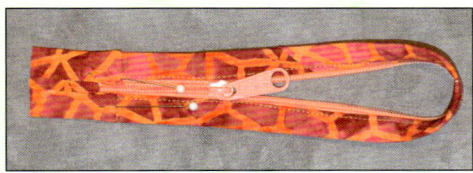

- Fold sides in and press.

- Fold end up, tucking the raw edge under and top stitch.

- Add hardware by clamping down with pliers or use a rubber mallet.

Zipper Lanyard

To make a lanyard to hold your glasses, name tag, or keys, a 10" square will give you a 36" long piece of bias. If you wish to have a longer lanyard, use a larger piece of fabric or two squares. Assemble as you would the key chain.

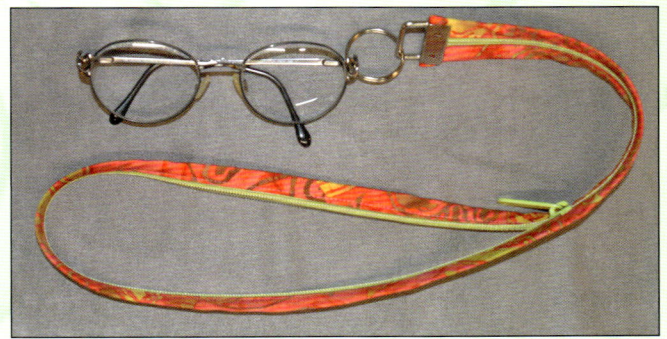

Quick Projects using Pre-cuts

ELECTRONICS BAG

I'm always in need of a sturdy bag to hold all my electronics cords. With a cell phone, tablet, laptop, earbuds and bluetooth, I'm always trying to keep track of cords and plugs. This bag keeps all my necessary cords together. This was made with Layer Cake® 10" squares of quilting cotton.

Supplies

- 4 Layer Cake® 10" squares
  (2 for the outside and 2 for the inside)

- 1 piece of fusible batting 10" x 16"

- One side zipper tape 20" and one slide

Construction

- Trim all four squares to 8" by 10".

- Sew two RST, along one 10" edge for inside and outside. (Make two)

- With the WST make a fabric sandwich with batting in the center.

- Fuse all three layers together. Quilt all three layers together as desired or use our helpful hints on page 50.

- This bag is sewn with French Seams so that there are no raw edges. For more info on French Seams, please refer to page 51.

- Fold in half, with lining to the inside, and sew a 1/4" seam allowance on ONE side only.

Fabric provided by Moda Fabric Handmade by Bonnie and Camille

Quick Projects using Pre-cuts

ELECTRONICS BAG (CONTINUED)

- Press seam toward one side, and turn inside out so the wrong sides are now out. Sew with a 3/8" seam allowance. Again, one side only!

- You will have one side open.

- Open bag top.

- With the zipper teeth down, sew one side of your zipper all along the top edge from one side to the other, right sides together, including sewing over side seam.

- Zig-zag or serge top edge to finish off any raw edges.

- Bring two ends of the zipper together and install slide on the end of the zipper.

- With WST, sew the remaining side with a 1/4" seam allowance.

- Turn wrong side out and press seam to one side.

- Sew a French Seam with right sides together with a 3/8" seam allowance. (See page 51.)

- Sew slowly at the top where you will be sewing over the zipper teeth. (Use a denim 100/16 needle.)

- Turn right side out, press flat and stuff with your cords!

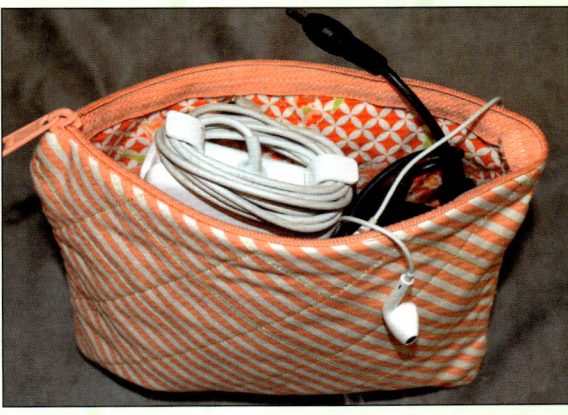

151

"ZIP IT" EYE GLASS CASE

This is a great 'scrap' project. It's also perfect for all of your extra 2½" strips! Quick, easy and they make great gifts! Thank you Linda Cooper for inspiring us with this project.

Supplies

- 2½" x 22" (2½" x 24" for larger eye glass frames) of fabric quilted with Super Shaping Foam®.
- 50" (55" for larger frames) zipper tape and one slide – separate the tape into two pieces. You only need one side of the tape for the eye glasses, so why not find another strip and another zipper slide and make one for a gift!
- 1" x 8" fabric strip folded and stitched to create a pull tab for the zipper. (See page 18.)
- Seven Corner Ruler®

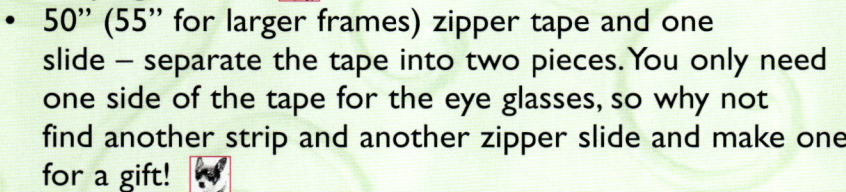

NOTE: I used fabric that was quilted on one side only. If you want your eye glass case lined with fabric, use Super Shaping Foam® Double Sided Fusible.

Construction

- With your serger, use a piping foot and a three thread narrow overlock stitch to trim a scant ¼" off of the zipper tape. (The narrower tape will turn much easier around the curves at the top and bottom.)

- With the Seven Corner Ruler®, mark a one inch curve on each side of each end of your fabric strip.

- Using the same narrow overlock stitch, stitch around the outside edge of your fabric strip to finish the raw edges. It may be necessary to lift the presser foot and physically turn the fabric a small amount at a time as you round the curves.

- If you do not have a serger, you will need to trim the zipper tape with a rotary cutter or scissors and stitch the edges of the tape and the quilted fabric with a zig zag stitch.

Fabric provided by Maywood Studios, Catalina Ultra Violet Collection

Quick Projects using Pre-cuts

"ZIP IT" EYE GLASS CASE (CONTINUTED)

- For the **smaller size**, **measure two inches** from the bottom of one end to mark where you will begin sewing the zipper to the fabric.

- **Measure three inches** from the bottom if making the **larger size**.

- Place zipper on the quilted fabric RST (zipper teeth down.)

- Be sure to leave at least an inch of zipper tape before you start. Begin sewing two or three inches from the bottom curve depending on the size you are making.

- Continue sewing until you reach your starting point.

- Leave a space of 1/2" between the beginning and the end of your sewing. This will give you enough room to attach the zipper slide.

- Attach zipper slide to the ends of the tape.

- Stitch across the open ends of the zipper tape to ensure they stay together.

- Fold bottom end up and pin to make it easier to get the zipper started.

- As soon as you have moved the zipper slide to the outside of the case, remove the pin and turn case to the outside.

- Continue zipping to the top.

- Tie the pull tab onto the zipper slide.

153

Quick Projects using Pre-cuts

STRAP WRAP

Supplies

- 5" x 6" quilted fabric
- 3" x 4" clear vinyl
- 5" hook and loop tape
- 25" x 2" for bias binding

Construction

- Stitch the vinyl pocket to center of the inside, stitching close to the edge of the sides and bottom.
- Stitch the hooks (the scratchy piece) to the top of the inside.
- Stitch the loops (the softer piece) to the bottom of the outside.
- Bind

**Fabric provided by Maywood Studios
Catalina Ultra Violet Collection
and Cuddle Suede
provided by Shannon Fabrics**

Quick Projects using Precuts

PRECUT PLAY

This is a great use of those precut fabric collections. And if you are prone to saving all of your fabric scraps, it is a great way to combine them into something fun and colorful!

Supplies
- Pre-cut fabric packs or fabric scraps of equal size. The piece pictured above is constructed with 2 $\frac{1}{2}$" squares.
- Fantastic Fusible Fabric Backing®.

NOTE: Fabric layout before stitching should be at least 25% larger that the finished piece you need.

Construction - *All seams are $\frac{1}{4}$".*
- Place Fantastic Fusible Fabric Backing® on the ironing board, fusible side up.
- Arrange fabric pieces on the backing. Make sure that all cut edges line up.
- Corner pieces will be either quarter square triangles or half square triangles depending on how many pieces you lay out.

- A ruler or a grid under the backing will help you keep the fabric pieces aligned.
- Fuse fabric to the backing.
- Fold fabric pieces together along the cut edges and stitch together with a 1/4" seam.
- Stitch all seams on one of the diagonals.
- Press seams to one side.
- Stitch seams on the other diagonal and press.
- You have now created a piece of fabric to use in your project.

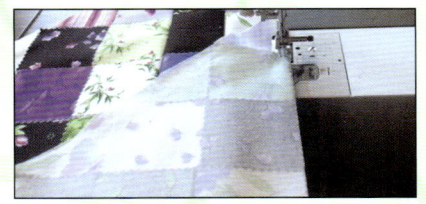

Fabric provided by Maywood Studios, Catalina Ultra Violet Collection

155

Quick Projects using Precuts

WINE BAG

It seems every time I'm invited to someone's house for dinner, I'm bringing a bottle of wine! Your token of appreciation will be that much more special if it's packed inside a pretty bag! Wine's not your thing: just resize the pattern pieces to make any size gift bag you need!

Supplies

- Outside 15"x12 ½" fabric you create using precuts (see page 155) or a solid piece of fabric.
- Inside lining 16"x12 ½" and 1½"x12 ½" for drawstring band.
- Drawstrings – 1" x WOF matching or coordinating with other fabrics used.
- Interfacing for outside if you are not using fabric you create with fabric pieces and backing.

Fabric provided by Maywood Studios Ultra Violet Collection

Construction - All seams are ½" unless otherwise noted.

- Stitch side and bottom seams of bag outside and lining.
- Box the corners of the outside and lining.
- On the bottom seam, measure 1" from the corner and fold the bottom seam onto the side seam at the mark. Stitch.
- Place lining inside the bag WST.
- Press down top edge of lining ½" and the press again ½" to encase top edge of the outside.

  NOTE: If the free arm on your machine is too large for the bag opening, the next steps will be much easier if you turn the bag inside out.

Quick Projects using Precuts

WINE BAG (CONTINUED)

Construction (CONTINUED)

- Top stitch along the edge of the lining.

- Stitch band seam for the first and last ½", leaving a ½" opening in the middle.

- Stitch a ½" buttonhole on band directly opposite from the seam opening.

- Press both top and bottom raw edges of the band ½" toward the wrong side of the fabric.

- For band placement, measure and mark 4" from the bag top.

- Align the top of the band with this line.

- Top stitch both edges of the band to the bag. (Top picture – No free arm. Bottom picture – using free arm of the machine.)

- Using the 1" x WOF fabric piece, create drawstrings using the directions on page 18 for Zipper Tabs.

- Cut into 2 equal pieces.

- Thread one tie in and out through the buttonhole opening in the band.

- Thread the other tie in and out of the seam opening in the band.

- Tie a knot with the two ends of each tie.

- Pull drawstrings to close the bag!

Bags that Hold More

Bags that Hold More

THE NEW AND IMPROVED EXPANDABLE ZIPPER BAG

This fun bag is actually a lesson in zipper installation techniques in disguise! You will learn 6 different zipper techniques while constructing this bag. These are techniques you will be able to use in pillows, cushions, slipcovers, duvet, back packs, luggage, and of course, hand bags!

Supplies

- 1 yard each of two coordinating fabrics.
- One package of Pam Damour Zipper Tape
- Matching thread
- Denim or jeans needle: size 100 or 16
- FriXion Pen
- Super Shaping Foam®: 15" x 27"
- Bonash Bonding Powder
- Basting tape
- Wooden yardstick
- 2" D-ring, or square ring
- 2" slider
- Deco-Magic®
- Swivel hook for optional key fob
- Double Welting or Zipper Foot
- Seven Corner Ruler®

Cutting

- Bag body: Cut 2 - 27" x 32" rectangle (one of each fabric)*
- Bag strap: Cut 1 - 6" x 42" (face fabric)
- Bag strap end: Cut 1 - 6" x 12" (face fabric)
- Pockets: Cut 2 - 7" x 17" (accent or lining fabric)
- Top Plackets: Cut 2 - 4" x 15 1/2" (one of each fabric)
- 2-way Zipper tabs: Cut 2 - 2" x 3", fabric of your choice.
- Super Shaping Foam®: 1 - 7" x 27", 2 - 4" x 27", 2 - 2" x 27"
- 1 1/4" yd 2 1/2" bias in lining or accent
- Deco-Magic®: 1 - 2" x 42", 1 - 2" x 12"

*When cutting a one-way directional fabric, cut 1" longer, and split along center. Seam fabric so the pattern is going in the right direction once the bag is folded in half.

Approx. finished size: 12" tall by 16" wide

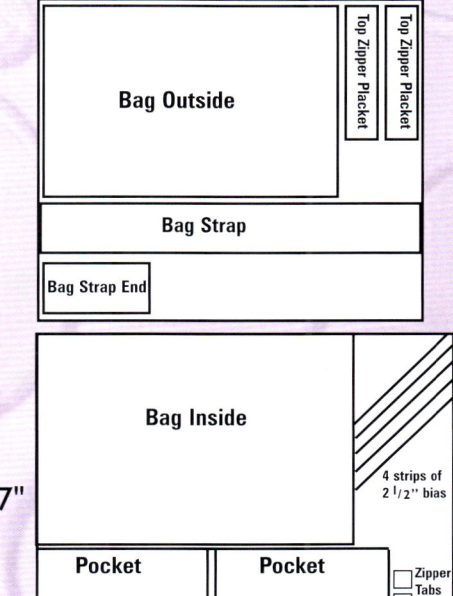

Fabric provided by Riley Blake, Apricot Floral Collection

Bags that Hold More

THE NEW AND IMPROVED EXPANDABLE ZIPPER BAG

(CONTINUED)

Bag Inside

Zipper Pocket

- On the top end of the wrong side of your zipper pocket, draw a 1/2" by 5 1/2" box, 1 1/2" down from the top edge, centering on the pocket.

- Draw a line down the center, making a "Y" at each end.

- With right sides together, pin the pocket top 1 1/2" from the top edge of the bag lining, centering it with about 12 1/2" on each side.

NOTE: You may do this by measuring the sides, or marking the center of each piece and line them up.

- Sew all the way around the box, starting along one of the long sides. Do not sew past the corner and do not back stitch. If you do, rip it out and start over.

- Cut down the middle of the box all the way to the "Y" at the corners. (See photo on page 21.)

- Pull all the pocket fabric to the back through the cuts and press flat.

- Cut 7" of zipper tape. Install zipper slide on your zipper tape, leaving both ends closed.

- Use basting tape or pins to position the zipper to the back of the pocket opening.

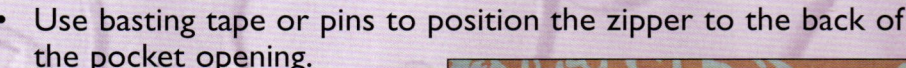

- Top stitch all the way around your zipper box opening to secure zipper.

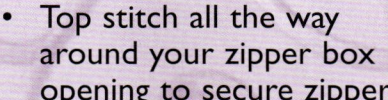

- Trim zipper ends if they extend more than a 1/2" from the end of the zipper box.

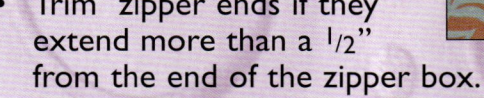

- Bring the pocket up to the top edge of the placket and sew the tops and sides.

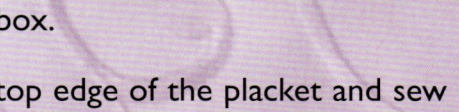

Bags that Hold More

THE NEW AND IMPROVED EXPANDABLE ZIPPER BAG
(CONTINUED)

Bag Outside
The bag outside is sewn similarly to the bag inside with a few minor differences.

- Fuse the 7" wide Super Shaping Foam® to the center of your bag face fabric, on the wrong side.

- On the outside pocket, draw your ½" x 5 ½" zipper box starting 2" down from the top.

- Center your pocket on the face fabric 1" down from the top edge.

- Sew zipper box on the line just as you did for the lining.

- Cut on each side of the center line. This will leave a thin amount of fabric and Super Shaping Foam® in the center. Cut this away.

- Pull the pocket fabric through the opening to the back. Allow the pocket fabric to wrap around the Super Shaping Foam® to create a "piping".

- Press the pocket opening. With basting tape on each side of the zipper, place the zipper on the back of the opening.

- Stitch in the ditch all the way around the zipper box.

Bags that Hold More

THE NEW AND IMPROVED EXPANDABLE ZIPPER BAG
(CONTINUED)

Bag Outside (CONTINUED)

- Trim off excess zipper tape, leaving 1/2" at each end.

- Fold the pocket in half, bringing the bottom edge even with the top.

- Sew the sides and top edges of pocket.

- Now that your pockets are completed, you are ready to start your bag assembly.

Bag Assembly

NOTE: *The 2 1/2" on each side are the bag ends. The zippers will be sewn in to each side of the 6" pleats.*

- Begin by fusing the 4" strips of the Super Shaping Foam® to the wrong side of the bag outside, leaving a 6" space and 2 ½" at each side.

- Then add add the 2" strip to each side, leaving 1/2" at each side. (The reason why each side is done in two pieces is because it helps the corners form nicely.)

- Pin the lining to the outside, wrong sides together with the zipper pockets at opposite ends. Sprinkle with Bonash Fusing Powder and press to fuse together.

Bags that Hold More

THE NEW AND IMPROVED EXPANDABLE ZIPPER BAG
(CONTINUED)

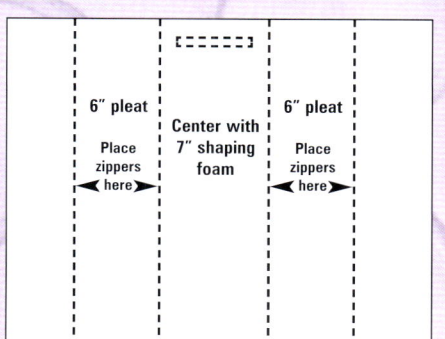

Bag Assembly (CONTINUED)

- On the right side, mark the outside bag fabric with your FriXion Pen, as shown here.

Expanding Zipper Insertion

- Cut two lengths of zipper tape the same length as fabric (27"), and separate zipper.

- Apply basting tape to the right side of your 4 zipper sections. With the zipper teeth down, and right sides together, line the teeth up with your line and finger press in place.

- With your double welting foot, sew all four sections of zipper in the same direction.

- Be mindful of how the pleats will fold after the zippers are in so that the zipper is sewn to the correct side of the fold. (see photo left)

- Using the rounded end of the zipper slide, start the slide onto the zipper, trying to keep the fabric ends as even as possible. After getting the slide on, slide all the way down and off the other end to close.

- Separate the end only about 3" or so and re-install slide leaving it mid-way on the bag with both ends of the zipper sealed.

- Fold your bag in half, with RST, and sew with a $1/2$" seam allowance.

- To finish your side seams, sew 2 $1/2$" bias with $1/2$" seam allowance. Fold raw edge of bias to raw edge of bag.

- Hold in place with basting tape.

THE NEW AND IMPROVED EXPANDABLE ZIPPER BAG
(CONTINUED)

Expanding Zipper Insertion (CONTINUED)

- Fold over to the stitching line and and top stitch.

Bag Bottom Corners

- Use the Seven Corner Ruler® to cut out the corner. Place on the 1 1/2" line and trim out corners.

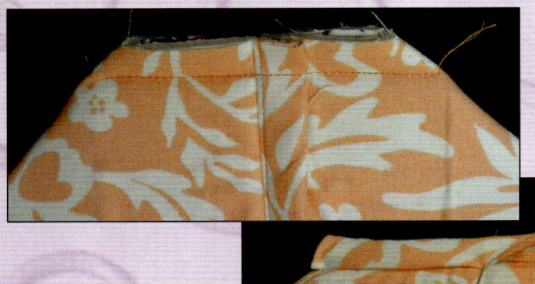

- Fold corners to look like this and sew closed.

- Sew 2 1/2" binding on seam.

Bag Strap

- On the center back wrong side, fuse your Deco-Magic Lite® to bag strap.

- Cut about 7" of zipper tape.

- Mark a line across the strap, 4" from the end. Separate zipper and with right sides together, sew as shown, starting about 4" from end at mark.

- Sew zipper with about a 3/8" seam allowance so the edge of the zipper tape will extend past the edge of the fabric.

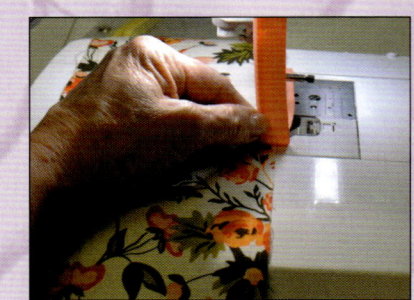

Bags that Hold More

THE NEW AND IMPROVED EXPANDABLE ZIPPER BAG
(CONTINUED)

Bag Strap (CONTINUED)

- With right sides together, marry zipper as shown. You will have to install slide twice so that the zipper will be closed at both ends.

- Finish strap by sewing edges together with a 1/2" seam allowance, with right sides together. Overlap zipper stitching by 1/2" on each end of zipper.

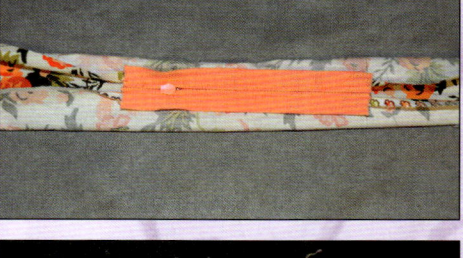

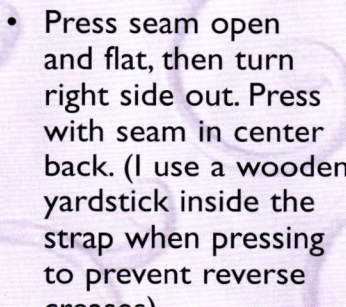

- Press seam open and flat, then turn right side out. Press with seam in center back. (I use a wooden yardstick inside the strap when pressing to prevent reverse creases).

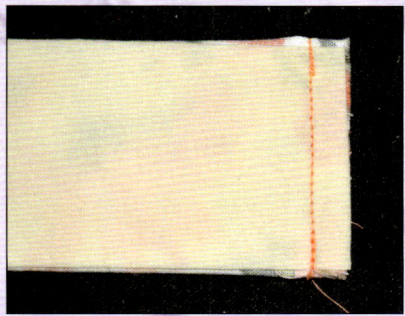

- Sew across the opposite end where you installed the zipper.

- Use your wooden yardstick to turn right side out. Press flat.

To make the Adjustable Strap turn to page 42.

Bag Strap End

- Fuse Deco-Magic Lite® centered on the wrong side of bag strap. Sew sides together and press seam open as you did for the strap. Sew across the end, turn right side out and press.

- Pull finished end through D-ring, fold over and sew down along edge.

- Sew each end of bag strap centered at each end of bag with 3/8" seam allowance.

Bags that Hold More

THE NEW AND IMPROVED EXPANDABLE ZIPPER BAG
(CONTINUED)

Two Way Top Zipper Placket
(For directions see page 23.)

- Pin top placket to the bag, along the inside edges.

- Pin the key fob in between the bag and placket, lining up along one end of placket. (See page 15 for directions on key fob.)

- Sew placket in place along the top edge with 3/8" seam allowance.

Finishing

- Sew your sections of 2 1/2" bias together. Leave ends with the diagonal cut.

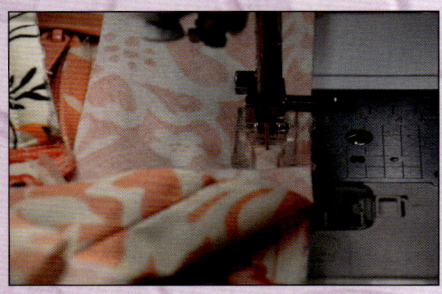

- Fold beginning end over 1/2". Pin and sew bias to the inside of bag, all the way around, starting at one end near the strap.

- When you get back to the beginning, overlap stitching about 1".

- Trim any excess at the same angle.

- Fold over bias so that the folded edge is just covering your stitching line. Top stitch in place.

Enjoy your new bag!

Optional Key Fob
(For directions see page 15.)

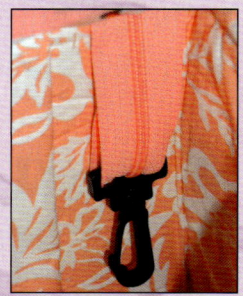

Bags that Hold More

THE WEEKENDER TOTE

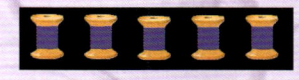

This may be the most useful bag you will ever create! As presented, it features seven outside pockets and four more on the inside of the bag. With the variations presented in the book, coupled with your own creativity, you will be able to create a bag that is truly yours.

The double zipper opening makes access a breeze and the size is perfect to hold all of your essentials for a quick weekend get away! Not traveling? No worries! It's a great tote for work or play!

Supplies

- 1 ¾ yds Outside fabric
- 2 yds Lining fabric (also used to accent the outside of the bag)
- 1 ¼ yds Coordinating fabric
- 36" x 58" package Super Shaping Foam Single Sided Fusible®
- 2 ½ yds. Zipper tape with 6 slides
- 2 ½ yds. Welt Cord
- 6" x 16" Deco-Magic®
- 1 Package bag feet
- Decorative thread for quilting and topstitching
- 25" x 10" piece of Heat'n Stay Lite® Fusible Batting for backing the outside front and side pockets

Fabric provided by Maywood Studios Catalina Ultra Violet Collection

Cutting and Quilting Instructions

- Cut and label all pieces. Instructions for each of the fabric layouts are written to the right of each diagram.

- 30" of the outside fabric fused to the Super Shaping Foam® and quilted. See page 50 for quilting instructions.

NOTE: Fabric will need to be turned 90° to fit on the foam for fusing.

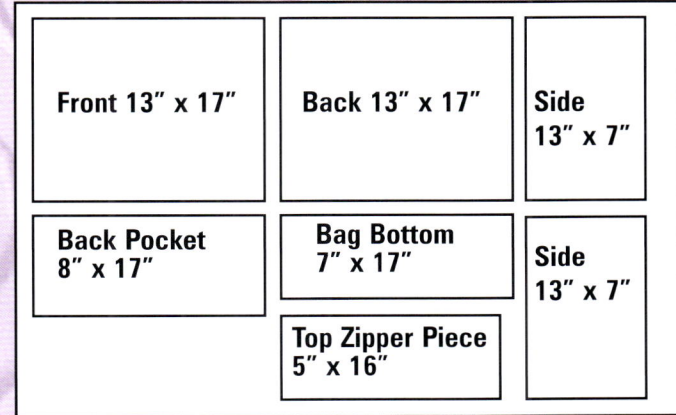

167

Bags that Hold More

THE WEEKENDER TOTE (CONTINUED)

Remaining Outside Fabric

- The side and front pockets need to be backed with batting and quilted. Use the Hanging Quilted Pocket piece to cut a matching piece from the Super Shaping Foam® and set aside.

| Side Pocket 7" x 9" | Side Pocket 7" x 9" | Front Pocket 9" x 9" | 9" x 17" Outside of Hanging Zipper Pocket |

8" x 19" for Hanging Quilted Pocket

Lining Fabric

- Once you have cut the 8" x 19" piece for the Hanging Quilted Pocket, be sure to layer it with the previously cut outside piece and Shaping Foam® piece. Quilt these together following directions used for the quilting the fabric for the outside of the bag.

| Side Pocket Backing 7" x 9" | Side Pocket Backing 7" x 9" | Front Pocket Lining 9" x 9" | Lining Inside Hanging Zip Pocket 9" x 17" |

16" x 23" Lining

5" x 16" Center Top Zip Lining
2" x 16" Side of Top Zip Closure
2" x 16" Side of Top Zip Closure
12" x 17" Center Zipper Pocket Lining

16" x 23" Lining

12" x 17" Center Zipper Pocket Lining

8" x 17" Back Carry Strap Pocket Lining

8" x 19" Lining for Inside Quilted Pocket

9" x 14" Buttonhole Pocket on Back Carry Strap

Inside Backing 9" x 8½"

Use this fabric to create bias trim required by pattern

Bags that Hold More

THE WEEKENDER TOTE (CONTINUED)

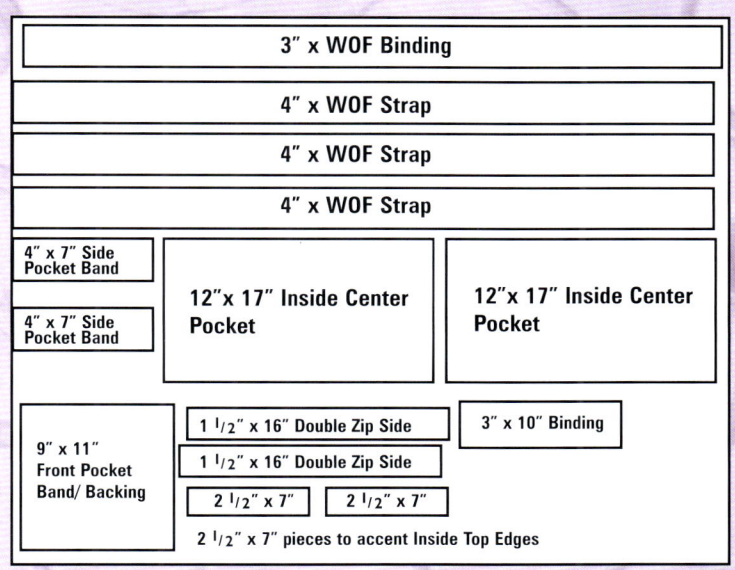

Coordinating Fabric

- Cut and label all pieces.

Construction - *All seams are 1/2" unless otherwise noted.*

- If you have not already quilted the outside fabric, side and front pockets and the fabric to be used for the Hanging Quilted Pocket, it's time to quilt!

Create Bias Fabric and Covered Welt Cord

- Use some of the remaining lining fabric to create a strip of bias fabric that measures 2" x 90". See page 10 to create bias.
- Cover Welt Cord with the bias fabric. (See page 55.)

Pocket directions are found in Bag Variations in this book. At this time, create all of the following pockets:

- Welt Trimmed Zipper Pocket page 35 for the outside front.
- 2 Welt Trimmed with Accent Band Pockets page 37 for the sides of the outside.

169

Bags that Hold More

THE WEEKENDER TOTE (CONTINUED)

Pockets (CONTINUED)

- Wide Carry Strap Pocket with the buttonhole zipper pocket included. Page 34 for the bag back. Use a 7" zipper box on the buttonhole pocket and 8" of zipper tape.

- Hanging Quilted Pocket page 31 for one side of the Bag Inside. Cut the 8" x 19" piece of quilted fabric into two pieces, one that is 7" x 9" and the other 5 1/2" x 9".

- Hanging Zipper Pocket page 29 for the other side of the bag inside.

- Dividing Zipper Pocket page 40 for the center of the inside.

Create the Straps

- Join the three strap sections with bias seams.

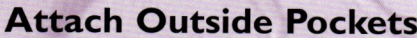

- From the remaining Super Shaping Foam®, cut 2 strips that measure 1" x the 58" length of the foam.

- Press the strap fabric piece in half lengthwise.

- Open and press each side toward the center.

- Open and lay the strips of foam between the center crease and one of the side creases.

- Fuse the foam in place.

- Fold and press again.

- Topstitch both sides of the Strap piece close to the outside edges and set aside.

NOTE: Topstitching is much easier if you stitch close to the fold before stitching the open edges together.

Attach Outside Pockets

- Welt Trimmed Zipper Pocket - Center this pocket on the lower edge of the bag front. Stitch 1/4" from the side and bottom edges to hold in place.

- Welt Trimmed with Band Pockets - Align one pocket with the lower edge of each bag side piece and with a 1/4" seam, stitch in place on the sides and lower edge of each pocket.

Bags that Hold More

THE WEEKENDER TOTE (CONTINUED)

Attach Outside Pockets (CONTINUED)

- Back Carry Strap Pocket - Mark a horizontal line 2 1/2" from the bottom edge of the bag back. Align the lower edge of the Carry Strap Pocket with this line.

- On the lower edge of the Carry Strap Pocket, measure 3 1/2" from each side and stitch in the ditch along the welt seam to create the bottom of the small side pockets on the Carry Strap Pocket.

Attach Straps

- Strap piece should measure 120"- 125" long. Cut 2 equal straps from this piece. You want them long enough to easily carry this bag on your shoulder. I like mine 54"- 58" each.

- On the bag front and the bag back, measure in 3" from each side and mark a line for the outside edges of the straps. Align the straps to this line. Make sure pocket edges are covered by the straps and caught in the topstitching.

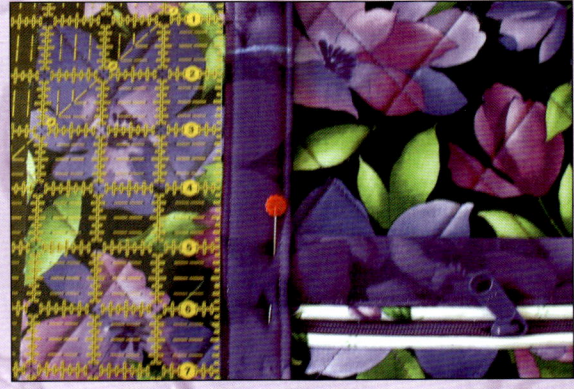

- Mark another line on each strap 1 1/2" from the top edge.

- Attach the straps to the bag front and back by topstitching on top of the stitching on each side of the straps and stitching across the marked line 1 1/2" from the top edge. You may want to stitch a 1" box with an 'X' at the top of each strap.

Bag Bottom

- Fuse the Deco-Magic® to the wrong side of the bag bottom.

- Attach the bag feet. (See page 14.)

Bags that Hold More

THE WEEKENDER TOTE (CONTINUED)

Create Outside

- Stitch bag sides to the bag bottom.

- Stitch bag front to side/bottom piece. Stitch from the top of one side down to the bottom, clipping at the corner of the side/bottom. Continue stitching across the bottom and up the other side in the same manner.

- Repeat for the bag back.

- Use some of the remaining lining fabric to create a strip of bias fabric that measures 2 1/4" x 55".

- Press in half and stitch to the outside top of the bag, joining with a mitered seam.

- Topstitch close to the folded edge.

Lining Construction

- Mark a 3" box on the lower corners of the front and back lining pieces.

NOTE: *The bottom edge of the lining measures 23" - be sure to mark the 3" boxes on each side of the bottom edge.*

- Cut and remove the marked corner boxes on both pieces of the lining.

- Stitch bottom lining seam.

- Press seam open.

- Pin one side of the Dividing Zipper Pocket to one side of a lining piece, setting the bottom edge of the pocket 1" above the cut corner.

Bags that Hold More

THE WEEKENDER TOTE (CONTINUED)

Lining Construction (CONTINUED)

- Stitch pocket where pinned.

- Pin and stitch the other side of the pocket to the other side of the lining piece in the same manner.

- Now pin and stitch the right side of the other lining piece to the right side of the first piece, sandwiching the pocket between the two pieces of lining.

- Press seams open.

- At the cut corners, align the side seams with the bottom seam and stitch a 1/2" seam across the cut corners.

- With both the lining and the outside turned inside out, align the bottoms so the stitched corners match.

- Stitch the lining and the bag outside together on these corner seams.

- Turn the outside of the bag right side out, inserting the lining into the outside at the same time.

- Make sure to align the center front and center back of the lining with the center front and center back of the bag.

- Pin or Wonder Clip® the top edge and stitch together with a scant 1/2" seam allowance.

- Center an inside hanging pocket on each side of the bag and stitch in place with a scant 1/2" seam allowance.

THE WEEKENDER TOTE (CONTINUED)

Finish the Top of the Bag

- Inside finishing pieces will create a finished look when you look at the top of the bag.

- With RST, fold side finishing pieces in half so they measure 2" x 7". Stitch a 1/2" seam on each end. Clip corners. Turn and press. Baste one to each side of the bag.

- Create Double Zipper Closure. (See page 16.)

- Pin or Wonder Clip® the Double Zipper Closure to the front and back sides of the inside top edge of the bag.

- Stitch in place with a scant 1/2" seam allowance.

- Stitch together the two 3" wide pieces of coordinating fabric that are marked 'binding'.

- Press seam open and press binding in half.

- Using the French Binding technique page 49, stitch the binding to the top of the inside of the bag using a 1/2" seam allowance.

- Use your favorite method of joining the binding.

- Press binding to the front and topstitch in place.

- Create and apply zipper tabs for the front, back pockets and the top closure. (See page 18.)

Bags that Hold More

WHEELED TOTE

Yes you can create a wheeled bag by yourself! This one makes a great carry on travel bag and it even holds a sewing machine!

Supplies

- 1 1/4 yd Outside fabric if it is 58"- 60" wide or 1 2/3 yd of 44" wide fabric
- 1 2/3 yd 44" Wide fabric for inside of the bag
- 45" x 60" of Super Shaping Foam® Double Sided Fusible for quilting the fabric
- 1/4 yd Super Shaping Foam® Single Sded Fusible or 4 1/2 yds of 2" foam strips for strap padding
- 1 2/3 yds Zipper tape with three slides
- 80" Standard Welt Cord
- 1 yd Coordinating fabric for straps, pocket lining and pocket trim
- 1/2 yd Accent fabric for bias trim, covering welt cord and binding inside seams
- Decorative thread for quilting and accent stitching
- 3/4 yd 1" Nylon webbing
- 3" Hook tape (the scratchy piece), 7" Loop tape (the fuzzy piece)
- 4 Wheels for the base, 16 - 3/4" hex screws to secure the wheels to the base
- 12" of 3/8" Plastic tubing
- Wood base - 1 piece of 3/4" plywood - no larger than 18 1/2" x 9 1/2" and no smaller than 18" x 9". Slightly round the corners to prevent excess wear.
- 24" x 14" Piece of fabric to cover the base - We used the outside suede used in the bag
- 24" x 14" Super Shaping Foam® or batting to pad the base
- Staple gun with 3/8" staples
- Wonder Clips
- Seven Corner Ruler®

Cuddle Suede fabric provided by Shannon Fabrics, trimming fabrics provided by Maywood Studios, Catalina Ultra Violet Collection

Construction

All Seams are 1/2" unless otherwise noted.

- Quilted fabric: Cut the 58" x 42" pieces of the outside fabric, lining fabric and Super Shaping Foam® into 3 pieces each - 2 - 58" x 12" and 1 - 58" x 17".

Bags that Hold More

WHEELED TOTE (CONTINUED)

Construction (CONTINUED)

All Seams are 1/2" unless otherwise noted.

- Layer three sets with outside fabric, foam and lining fabric and quilt using directions on page 50.

- Use the diagram to the right to cut pattern pieces from the quilted fabric pieces.

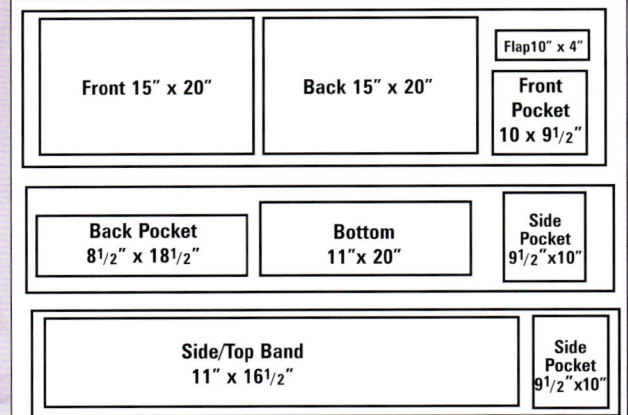

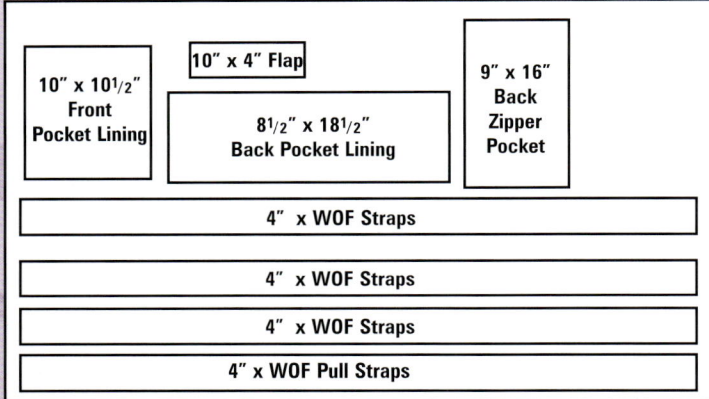

- Label all pattern pieces.

- Cut the coordinating fabric using the diagram to the left. Cut and label all pieces.

- Using the accent fabric, follow the directions on page 10 to create bias trim. You need the following strips of bias: 80" x 2 1/2" to bind inside seams, 80" x 2" to cover welt cord, 225" x 2" to create bias trim for seam and zipper edges.

- Cover 80" of Welt Cord with the 80" x 2" piece of bias. See page 55. Use as directed for pockets and seam insertions.

- Use the 3" Curve on the Seven Corner Ruler® to curve the top corners of the bag front and bag back.

- Side Pockets - follow directions on page 37 to create two Welt Trim with Accent Band pockets.

- Center a pocket on each end of the side/top band. Stitch in place on the bottom with a scant 1/2" seam.

Bags that Hold More

WHEELED TOTE (CONTINUED)

Construction (CONTINUED)

- Baste the side edges of the pockets to the side/top band close to the raw edges of the pocket pieces.

- Create back pocket following the directions on page 34 for the Wide Carry Strap Pocket. Use an 8" box and 9" of zipper tape for the included Buttonhole Zipper Pocket.

- To attach the back pocket, align the bottom of the pocket 4" from the bottom edge of the bag and stitch in place by stitching in the ditch along the welt cord. Stitch pocket sides close to the raw edges of the pocket.

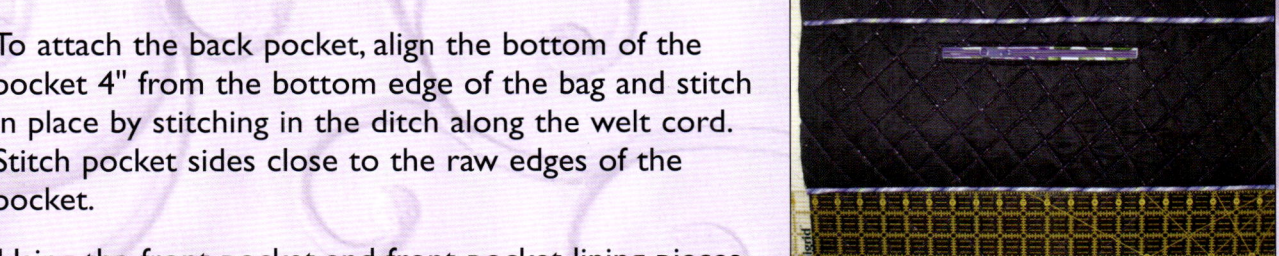

- Using the front pocket and front pocket lining pieces follow directions on page 41 to create the front pocket with Easy Binding.

- Center pocket on bag front. Stitch in place on the sides and bottom of the pocket, stitching close to the raw edges.

- To create the front and back straps, join the 3 strap pieces into one long strip using bias seams. Using the directions for padded straps on page 45, add a 2" wide strip of Single Sided Fusible Super Shaping Foam® to the center of the strap fabric and press and stitch as directed.

- Cut this strap section into 2 equal pieces to be used as front and back straps.

- Straps should be placed 4 1/2" from each side.

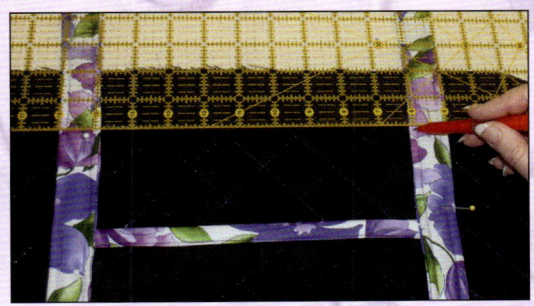

- Stitch in place by stitching on top of the stitching used to create the strap, and stopping 2" from the top of the bag. Create a 1" box with an 'X' stitched in the middle at the top of each strap. This will help to reinforce the strap.

WHEELED TOTE (CONTINUED)

Construction (CONTINUED)

- Use the 1 1/2" curve on the Seven Corner Ruler® to curve the lower corners of the pocket flap and pocket flap lining.

- Apply covered Welt Cord to the sides and bottom edges of the pocket flap. (See page 55.)

- Stitch the flap lining to the flap RST along the side and bottom edges.

- Turn right side out and press.

- Serge or zigzag stitch the open top edges together.

- Center flap above the front pocket keeping the edge of the flap 3/4" from the top of the pocket.

- Stitch in place with a 1/4" seam allowance.

- Press flap down toward the pocket and topstitch in place 1/4" from the fold.

- Apply bias trim to the long sides of the band and the side and top edges of the front and back, following directions on page 54.

- As you serge or zigzag stitch the edges of the bias trim, be sure to also finish the bottom edges of the front and back pieces of the bag in the same manner.

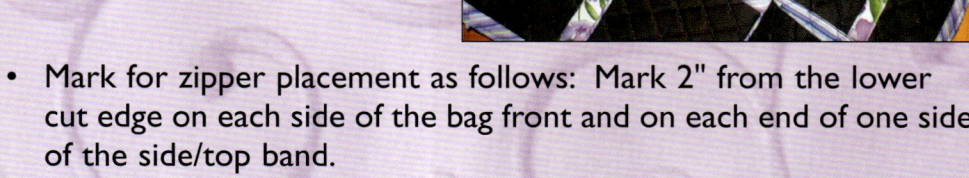

- Mark for zipper placement as follows: Mark 2" from the lower cut edge on each side of the bag front and on each end of one side of the side/top band.

- Stitch the zipper Tape to the side/top band RST between these marks making sure to leave an extra 1 1/2" of tape beyond the stitching at each end. (You need this extra zipper tape to attach the zipper slides and create stops for the zipper ends).

Bags that Hold More

WHEELED TOTE (CONTINUED)

Construction (CONTINUED)

- This has now attached one side of the zipper tape to the band and given you the correct amount of zipper tape to apply to the bag front.

- Separate the zipper tape and pin or Wonder Clips the other half to the bag front as follows: Align the middle of the tape with the top center of the bag front and then pin or Wonder Clip the lower ends at the 2" mark again leaving 1 1/2" of tape extending past the marks.

- Now pin or Wonder Clip the zipper tape along the straight edges of the top and sides.

- You will now need to force the tape to fit along the curves at the rounded corners of the bag front. You will be stitching fairly close to the zipper teeth and this will make it possible to stitch these curves without clipping into the zipper tape! Really, you can do it. If you find you have just too much zipper, ease a little of it into the straight edges.

- Stitch zipper in place on bag front.

- Turn zipper to the inside on the front and band. Press to the inside.

- On the front and on the band, topstitch on the bias trim close to the folded edge near the zipper teeth.

- Apply covered welt cord to the short edges of the band at the bottom of the pockets.

- Stitch the bag bottom to the top/side band on each side. Trim seam to 1/4" and bind with French binding technique on page 49.

- Create the pull handle for the Wheeled Bag and attach to one side of the top/side band.

179

Bags that Hold More

WHEELED TOTE (CONTINUED)

Construction (CONTINUED)

- Use the 4" x WOF strip you cut for the handle. (If you are taller than 5'7" you may want to make this handle a bit longer. You can test length by pinning a mock handle on the bag to determine needed length.)

- Center the Super Shaping Foam® 2" x 45" strip (will need to be longer if you have lengthened the handle) on the fabric strip. Fuse. Press remaining fabric over the foam, and then press the strip in half.

- Open up and stitch the short ends together with a 1/4" seam, trimming the foam from the seam allowance. Press seam open.

- Re-fold and topstitch close to the long folded edge.

- Place pins to divide into 2 equal pieces.

- At each end, where you have placed the marking pins, place another pin 3 1/2" on each side of those first pins. This will mark a 7" section of the strap centered at each end.

- Topstitch the open side of the strap, starting at the beginning of one 7" section, continuing along one side of the strap and ending when you have stitched the other 7" section closed.

- You should now have the two 7" sections stitched closed, as well as the side of the strap connecting them and with the other long side left open.

- Stitch through the width of the strap at the pins marking the closed end of each 7" section. This will give you a stop point for the tubing.

- Cut the 12" of plastic tubing in half creating two 6" pieces.

- Insert one 6" piece of tubing into one of the 7" sections.

- Stitch a vertical stop point at the open end of this 7" section.

Bags that Hold More

WHEELED TOTE (CONTINUED)

Construction (CONTINUED)

- Starting at this vertical stop point, topstitch all but 2" of the remaining long opening along the side of the strap.

- On one side of the top/side band, mark a line 3" above the top of the side pocket and center the other 7" section over this mark.

- Stitch the strap to the side on top of the topstitching.

- You should have a small opening in the strap that will need to be hand stitched closed.

- Pin or Wonder Clip the bag back to the bag bottom.

- Stitch in place.

- Stitch a bar tack at the closed end of the strap to reinforce the strap.

- Insert the other piece of tubing through the open end of the strap.

- Bar tack that end.

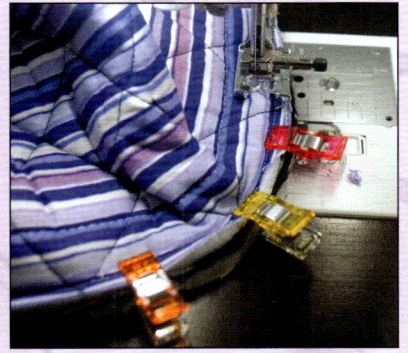

- Pin or Wonder Clip the sides and top of the bag back to the band, clipping the band at the seams where the band attaches to the bottom.

- Stitch together with the band on top.

- Cut 10" of webbing and stitch the 3" of loop tape to one end.

181

WHEELED TOTE (CONTINUED)

Construction (CONTINUED)

- Cut 15" of webbing and stitch the 7" of hook tape to one end.

- Stitch the longer piece of webbing to the center of the bottom seam in the back of the bag.

- Trim the bag back, bag bottom and band seam allowances to $1/4$" and using the 2 $1/2$" bias strips bind the seam allowance following directions on page 49.

- Stitch the bag front to the bag bottom and to the lower 1 $3/4$" of each side of the side/top band, clipping the corners as needed.

- Stitch the shorter piece of webbing to the center of the bottom seam on the front of the bag.

NOTE: *Make sure that the extra ends of the zipper tape do not get caught in the stitching.*

- Working with the bag turned inside out, attach zipper slide to one end of the zipper tape and zip it on and right off again. This will close the zipper.

- Attach a zipper slide to each end of the zipper. Leave some of the center open so you can use the slides to open the bag after covering the ends of the zipper.

- Cover the ends of the zipper tape with a small piece of fabric to provide a stop for the zipper and to give a finished look to the zipper ends.

- Turn Bag right side out.

- Stitch Zipper tabs. (See page 18.) Tie onto front zipper slides and back pocket zipper slide.

Now it's time to make the bottom platform and attach the wheels.

- Cover one side of the plywood base with the Super Shaping Foam® or batting wrap to the underside of the plywood trimming corners as needed. Staple in place.

- Repeat with the fabric cover.

- Place the covered base into the bag and attach the wheels to the bottom of the outside with $3/4$" hex screws.

Acknowledgements

Thank you to the following companies who provided us with support through their products and machines. We hope you will thank these companies by supporting them.

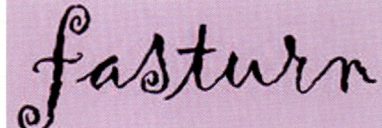

Embroidery

184

Glossary

NOTE: *You'll find terms here not in this book, but I included them so you could use this as a reference guide for all your sewing projects.*

Basting
Temporary stitches used to create gathers, or to temporarily sew something together. The stitches are usually 3.5-4.5mm in length and are taken out when the project is completed.

Basting in the Hoop
This is also known as fixing in the hoop. It is done in the embroidery function/mode of your sewing machine and is a series, usually a square or rectangle, of basting stitches. These stitches outline your design area as well as tack layers of fabric or stabilizers together.

Bias
If something is cut on the true bias, it is cut at 45 degrees to the selvage or at a diagonal line across the fabric.

Bias Band
A strip of fabric cut on the bias, and applied onto another fabric.

Binding
A method for finishing edges or seams by wrapping fabric over the edge to encase the raw edges.

Fabric Grain
The direction of the fabric, up and down the length or perpendicular to the selvedge. They are called the lengthwise grain, crosswise grain and the bias.

Fantastic Fusible Fabric Backing
60" wide light weight sheer fusible stabilizer designed to stabilize fabric without changing the hand of the fabric.

French Binding
Similar to Binding, but fabric is folded in half before wrapping.

FriXion Pen
This pen, not designed for fabric use, is used by many sewists. It gives a crisp line and disappears when ironed. Fabric needs to be washed to remove pen residue.

Hemostats
A locking pair of pliers similar to needle nose. They are usually used as a clamp in the medical field.

Hook & Loop Tape
Known by its brand name, Velcro®.

Kraft•Tex™
A thick leather looking paper that is very durable and can be used in sewing projects.

Lining
This is a lightweight fabric that lines a project. It prevents lighter weight fabrics from being too sheer as well. Linings can complement the outside fabric or contrast for an exciting inside personality to your project.

Miter
The technique when binding a project that results in 45 degree corners on a right angle.

Piping
A decorated or covered cording inserted into the seam of a project for decoration; also known as welting.

Pivot
Turning a corner or angle while your needle is in the fabric and the presser foot is raised to prevent fabric from shifting.

Placket
An extra piece of fabric added to hold a zipper.

Raw Edge
The cut edge of a project. It may fray or ravel if left in this state.

Glossary

RFID Fabric
Used to line wallets and bags to prevent thiefs from scanning critical credit card and identity data.

Right Side (RS)
Right side, usually in reference to the right side of fabric, which is the side of the fabric with the print or finish.

Right Side Together (RST)
Right sides together. A term meaning that two pieces of fabric should have the right sides facing each other before you sew.

Sandwich
The method of layering fabrics, batting, and/or stabilizer together before sewing.

Seam Allowance (SA)
The fabric between the cut edge of the project and the seam line. This measurement varies based on the type of project you are doing. This book was written with the standard 1/2" seam allowances, unless otherwise specified.

Seam Ripper
A sewer's best friend! Used to remove basting stitches as well as "accidents".

Selvage
The woven edge of the fabric. One of the selvages usually has printing on it.

Stiletto
This tool is your "third hand" when sewing. It's very sharp, can hold your fabric in place as you sew, and won't damage the fabric.

Straight Grain
The direction of the threads traveling parallel to the selvage.

Super Shaping Foam®
By The Decorating Diva, Super Shaping Foam comes 60" wide and can be purchased as single sided fusible or double sided fusible.

Top Stitching
A decorative stitch like edge stitching, but further from the edge of the garment. It can come in multiple rows and looks very nice.

WOF
Width of Fabric

Wonder Clips
By Clover, these clips take the place of pins and are great to hold fabric edges together. They come in assorted sizes to accommodate different weights of fabrics.

Wrong Side (WS)
Wrong side, usually in reference to the wrong side of fabric. This side of the fabric is bland and usually has a muted version of the print side of the fabric.

Wrong Sides Together (WST)
Wrong sides together, the two fabrics that are to be sewn together have the wrong sides of the fabric touching.

These are the Clover products we love and used in the book.

Product List

The follow are available at www.pamdamour.com

- Adjustable Bag Strap Hardware
- 60" Bag Chain
- Bag Feet
- Basting Tape
- Bonash Fusing Powder
- Brass Seam Ripper
- Brass Stiletto
- Continuous Bias Guide
- Double Sided Basting Tape
- Fantastic Fusible Fabric Backing®
- Fasturn Tube Turner
- FriXion Pen
- Heat Cutting Tool
- 10" Macro Wallet Clasps
- Micro Welt
- Permanent Double Stick Tape
- RFID Fabric
- 5-in-1 Ruler
- Sew Sisters Seven Corner Ruler
- Size 00 Phillips Head Screwdriver
- Small Wallet Clasps
- Snip It Scissors
- Super Shaping Foam (Comes in Single or Double Sided Fusible)
- Swivel Clip
- 7 1/2" Wallet Clasps
- Welt Cord
- Zipper Tape and Slides
- Wonder Clips

Index

A
Acknowledgements, 183
Adjustable Strap, 42
Appliqué Embroidery, 8
Art Supply Wallet, 96

B
Bag Feet, 14
Bag Straps, 42
Bags that Hold More, 158
Basic Instructions, 7
Basic Zipper Insertion, 25
Bias Binding, 47
Bias (create), 10
Bias Trim, 54
Binding, 47
Box Corners, 26
Brush on Fabric Coating Gel, 53
Buttonhole Zipper Insertion, 21
Buttonhole Zipper Pocket, 38

C
Card Pockets, 93
Card and Top Pocket Assembly, 93
Clutch & Wallet Clasp Frames, 12
Continuous Bias, 10
Corners, 26

D
De-De's Bag, 107
Dividing Zipper Pocket, 40
Double Folded Padded Strap, 46
Double Zipper Closure, 16

E
Easy Binding Pocket, 41
Electronics Bag, 150
Elegant Organizer, 97
Embroidery Designs on CD, 184
Embroidery Basics, 7
Essential Travel & Cosmetic Bags, 131
Evening Clutch, 96

F
Fabric Coating Gel, 53
Fantastic Fusible Fabric Backing, 7
Foreword, 6
French Binding, 49
French Seams, 51

G
Glossary, 185
Grab-n-Go Make Up Bag, 139
Great Finishes, 47

H, I
Hanging Quilted Pocket, 31
Hanging Zipper Pocket, 29
Hardware, 12
Heat Dissolving Stabilizers, 8
Hold Anything Basket, 70
Hold Everything Bag, 58

J
Jaclyn's Bag, 112

K
Key Fobs, 15
Kraft•Tex™ Piped Strap, 44

L
Laminating Fabric, 52
Leigh's Yoga Bag, 116

Index

M
Machine Quilting with the Seven Corner Ruler®, 50
Macro Wallet, 75
Math Formulas for Calculating Continuous Bias, 11
Melinda Bag, 119
Men's Toiletry Bag, 141
Micro Welt, 55-56
Mini Wallet, 87
Monogram Embroidery, 9

N
New and Improved Expandable Zipper Bag, 159

O
Odicoat, 53
Open Buttonhole Zipper Pocket, 39
Organizers, 57

P
Padded Strap, 45
Peel & Stick Stabilizer, 7
Piped Strap, 43
Pocket Wallet, 89
Pocket with Welt Trim and Accent Band, 37
Pockets, 28
Precut Play, 155
Pressing Laminating Fabric, 52
Product List, 187

Q
Quick Clutch Wallet, 92
Quick Projects using Pre-Cuts, 147

R
Rounded Box Corners, 27
Round Corners, 28

S
Seven Corner Ruler®, 28, 50
Sew on the Go, 130
Sewing Welt or Piping onto Fabric, 55
Splicing Cord, 56
Stabilizer, 7
Strap Wrap, 154
Straps, 42-46

T, U, V
Teacher's Pet, 123
Tear Away Stabilizers, 8
Three Dimensional Embroidery, 8
Travel Roll Up, 136
Two Way Top Zipper Placket, 23, 162

W, X, Y
Wallet Clasp, 12
Water Tote, 143
Wash Away Stabilizers, 8
Weekender Tote, 167
Welt Cord, 55
Welt Trim Zipper Pocket, 35
Wheeled Tote, 175
Wide Carry Strap Pocket, 34
With a Little Help from our Friends, 106
Wine Bag, 156
Wristlet Key Chain, 148

Z
Zip It Eye Glass Case, 152
Zipper End Tabs, 24
Zipper Lanyard, 149
Zipper and Seam Trim, 54
Zipper Pocket Bag, 103
Zipper Tabs, 18
Zipper Tape Key Fob, 15
Zippered Lining, 19
Zippers, 16

Notes